CHRISTIAN ENCOUNTERS

ISAAC
NEWTON

CHRISTIAN ENCOUNTERS

ISAAC NEWTON

MITCH STOKES

THOMAS NELSON
Since 1798

NASHVILLE   DALLAS   MEXICO CITY   RIO DE JANEIRO

Published in Nashville, Tennessee, by Thomas Nelson. Thomas Nelson is a registered trademark of Thomas Nelson, Inc.

Thomas Nelson, Inc., titles may be purchased in bulk for educational, business, fund-raising, or sales promotional use. For information, please e-mail SpecialMarkets@ThomasNelson.com.

Library of Congress Cataloging-in-Publication Data

Stokes, Mitch.
  Isaac Newton / by Mitch Stokes.
    p. cm.
  Includes bibliographical references (p.   ).
  ISBN 978-1-59555-303-4
  1. Newton, Isaac, Sir, 1642-1727. 2. Scientists—Great Britain—Biography. 3. Science—Philosophy. 4. Newton, Isaac, Sir, 1642-1727—Religion. I. Title.
  QC16.N7S76 2010
  530.092—dc22
  [B]
                              2009043322

Printed in the United States of America

09 10 11 12 HCI 6 5 4 3 2 1

TO MY GRANDMOTHER,
PAULINE HARBER

CONTENTS

1

A POSTHUMOUS SON

Isaac Newton could still feel the dull ache in his stomach where Arthur Storer had kicked him on the way to school that morning. At twelve or thirteen years old, Isaac was small for his age. Slumped at his desk in the back of the class, he could see the older and larger boy who not only sat ahead of him in the classroom, but held a higher spot in the school's academic rankings. Once in a while one of the students would turn back and look at him; he could feel his ears burn. Newton knew that if Arthur went unchallenged, there would likely be further beatings. Boys smell fear, and some of them feed on it. Newton would have to do something. The pain in his gut was replaced by the fluttering of butterflies.

After school Isaac challenged Arthur to settle things in the churchyard next to the school. The two were followed by the rest of the boys who, like boys throughout the ages, simply couldn't resist. Isaac had something to prove and was intent on doing so. At the very least, he would defiantly take as much as the older boy could dish out. That would at least make Arthur—and the others—think twice before picking on him again. But by that time, Newton's fear had built into a violent fury, and it was Arthur who received the beating. Shocked by Isaac's ferocity, Arthur submitted and gave up, something Isaac would never do. The headmaster's son—a much older boy—pointed out that Arthur was a coward for giving up and, according to the rules of engagement, Isaac must treat him as such. Isaac complied and took Arthur by the ears, dragging his face across the stone wall, leaving a message for all to see.

Arthur must have been taken entirely by surprise. Isaac—in addition to his small physical stature—was socially slight. He was quiet and removed, playing mostly alone. One of his few school friends described him as a "sober, silent, thinking lad." No one would have guessed that there was fire beneath his skin.

And the fight fueled this flame. At the time, not only was he ranked behind Storer; he was second to last out of eighty or so students. (As Newton later admitted, he was "very negligent"[1] in his schoolwork.) With the fight over, however, Isaac announced that he would pass Arthur in the rankings. This was a task for which Newton was naturally gifted; what he lacked in physical stature, he more than made up for intellectually. He overtook Arthur and rose quickly through the ranks of students, carving his name on every desk as he moved to the front. Positioned at the head of the school, it would be where he remained.

Were it not for this fight, in all likelihood Newton would have become a farmer. The incident is Newton's story in miniature. Throughout his life, Newton nurtured his solitude, cultivating his ideas by spending his hours in isolated contemplation. He was happiest when alone with books, papers, experiments, and ideas.

When asked once how he had come up with his law of universal gravitation, he answered, "By thinking on it continually."[2] This was one of the keys to his successes. He also remarked that truth is "the offspring of silence and unbroken meditation."[3] He mostly shunned the company of others in order to focus his energies on discoveries and developments. Only at the encouragement of a few close colleagues would he make these discoveries known to the outside world. He wrote millions upon millions of words in his lifetime but published only a fraction of them. And whenever debates over his theories arose—which frequently happened given their novel nature—he was at first reluctant to engage. But when he did engage, he was deadly. Heaven help the man who opposed him with charges of plagiarism or carelessness or incompetence.

Newton was tenacious when attacking problems as well, whether in mathematics, physics, theology, or chemistry. When gripped by a puzzle, he became obsessive, continually assailing it until it finally succumbed, which it usually did. Were it not for his intensity and focus, Newton would never have made the progress he did. Like ordinary mortals, he would have been stymied. His fortitude, perseverance, and ability to focus were—on his own admission—even more important than his innate intellectual capacity. At his birth, however, any strength he possessed—physical, mental, or otherwise—was hidden.

Newton was born on Christmas Day in a small upstairs bedroom of his family's manor house in Woolsthorpe, England. It was 1642, at least by England's reckoning (England's calendar was roughly ten days out of sync with the Continent's). Galileo died that same year.

Isaac was born several weeks prematurely, very small, and

very sick. The attending nurses were sent to the next town for medicine, but despite the seriousness of the situation, they stopped along the way to rest because they were sure that the baby was as good as dead. Yet he survived the night. And the next day. And the day after that. Each day, he precariously clung to life, his mother, Hannah, postponing his baptism in nearby Colsterworth for a week, while Isaac slowly gained strength. He was so small he could fit into a "quart pot." And small he would remain; even as an adult he was short. While an infant, he was fitted with a special neck brace so he could breathe and nurse properly. But he would not remain sickly and lived eighty-four more years.

"Isaac" was not a "son of laughter" (one of his secretaries said later that he had only seen him laugh once); rather he was named after his father. But the senior Isaac Newton ("New Town") had died a few months earlier, in October—only six months after his marriage to Hannah. He was only thirty-six. Of what he died, we don't know, but his death was not entirely unexpected. A few days earlier, he wrote in his will that he was of sound mind but ill body. And so, in the space of a few months, Colsterworth's parish registry listed three major family events for the Newtons: a death, a birth, and a baptism (the latter entry was, "Isaac sonne of Isaac and Hanna Newton Baptized Jan. 1"[4]). Newton was a "posthumous" son, born after the death of his father.

Newton's father—a yeoman, or upper-class farmer—left more than his name to his son. He bequeathed to him the two-story stone farmhouse of Woolsthorpe manor and a hundred acres of surrounding farmland, as well as a number of cottages and tenant farmers. In addition, Isaac inherited 234 sheep ("Woolsthorpe" means "wool farm") and 46 cattle, a considerable number of both.

At least financially, Isaac Sr. left his pregnant wife and unborn child very comfortable. Isaac was born as the lord of Woolsthorpe manor and was expected to be a yeoman like his father, which carried with it a certain power of authority, including the authority to fine villagers for minor breaches of law.

It was expected, therefore, that his mother would provide Newton with the same kind of education his father had—namely none. Isaac Sr. was illiterate and signed his name with his "mark," the traditional *X*. Hannah was from the Ayscough (or Askew) family, of genteel status, and so a bit higher up on the social ladder than her husband. Nevertheless, she received a minimal education, typical for women of her position. She, at least, could sign her name (as evidenced by her signature on her will). The one surviving letter we have of hers, which she wrote to her son while he was at Cambridge, reveals the limited training she received (the paper is torn, so some words are missing):

> Isack
>
> received your letter and I perceive you
>   letter from mee with your cloth but
>   none to you your sisters present thai
>   love to you with my motherly lou
>   you and prayers to god for you I
>
> your loving mother
> hanah
> wollstrup may the 6. 1665 [5]

We do not know much about Hannah's background, not even her birth date. We know more about her brother, the Reverend William Ayscough, who looked after Hannah and Isaac, and would be instrumental in setting Newton on his academic course. Ayscough was an Anglican rector (leader or director) of a parish two miles from Woolsthorpe. He received his MA from Trinity College at Cambridge University, where Isaac would eventually attend.

When Newton was three years old, Hannah (probably around thirty years old) caught the attention of Barnabas Smith, the sixty-three-year-old rector of nearby North Witham. Smith's first wife had died sixth months earlier, and Smith felt it was high time to get on with what was left of his life. A parishioner recommended Hannah as "an extraordinary good woman"[6] with fine prospects. Smith, not having the courage to face possible rejection in person, sent the parishioner to propose for him, paying him a day's wage for his trouble.

Understandably not swept off her feet, Hannah replied that she would have to consult her brother William before answering. As a widow with a young son and an estate to maintain until he was ready to take it over, she perhaps felt that there was more here to consider than love. Smith was very wealthy. A large inheritance had provided far more than what he received as rector. And as anyone who has read Jane Austen knows, this union would benefit the Ayscough family as well. On the advice of William, if not her heart, Hannah accepted Smith's proposal with two conditions: that Isaac be left a parcel of Smith's land and that Smith renovate the Woolsthorpe manor, which had fallen into disrepair. Smith agreed, but added his own condition: Hannah would come and live with him in North Witham—without Isaac.

Surprisingly (to us at least), Hannah accepted. Perhaps she reasoned that, given the advancement in Isaac's own prospects, as well as the high probability that Smith had little time left to live, on the whole, the arrangement would benefit her son. In any case, her mother, Margery, came to Woolsthorpe to care for Isaac while Hannah moved to her new home a mile and a half away. Later, if young Newton climbed a tree, he could see the steeple of North Witham's church. His mother was near, but not near enough.

We don't know how often Newton saw his mother. We do know that she would sometimes visit for an afternoon. And Newton didn't often attend the worship services of his stepfather, but rather he and his grandmother would ride to Colsterworth's fourteenth-century church, where he had been baptized, and in whose cemetery his father and grandfather were buried.

Smith lived eight more years and fathered three children with Hannah. When he died—Newton was now ten years old—she returned to Woolsthorpe, arriving with an increase in both property and children. And Hannah Ayscough Newton Smith had gained one more name.

Isaac's reunion with Hannah didn't last long. Until that time, he attended two local schools, called "dame schools" because they were named after their headmistresses. Perhaps Newton was being educated on the advice of William Ayscough (and maybe even his stepfather, who himself was an Oxford graduate). In any case, the dame schools were close enough that Isaac could walk back and forth each day. When he turned twelve, however, it was decided that he needed more than the village schools could provide. Newton was therefore sent to school in Grantham, a market town seven miles away. Seven miles was too far for him to remain in Woolsthorpe, so Newton packed his school supplies and moved to Grantham.

One of Hannah's friends was married to Grantham's apothecary, Joseph Clark. Newton was allowed to board in the Clark family's attic. Mrs. Clark had three children from a previous marriage, Edward, Arthur, and Catherine Storer. We have met Arthur. Arthur's sister, Catherine Storer, would, later in life, be a helpful source of information about Newton's years at Grantham. She was one of the two children he counted as friends during his school days. In fact, Catherine later recalled that she and Newton were more than friends; he had held her hand. He may have later considered marrying her. Newton's nineteenth-century biographer, Sir David Brewster, wrote that Miss Storer "seems to have added to great personal attractions more than the usual allotment of female talent,"[7] which is apparently a compliment. Catherine and Isaac never married—she said Newton's life of scholarship made marriage imprudent. They did, however, remain friends, and Newton would visit her and her husband when in Grantham. Brewster said that Newton even "liberally relieved her from little pecuniary embarrassments which seem to have occasionally beset her family."[8]

Catherine recalled that the other boys resented Newton because he was intellectually superior. By her account, he "never was known scarce to play with the boys abroad."[9] Rather, he usually preferred his own company or, sometimes, the company of girls. We wouldn't expect this to endear him to the other boys, and Newton's aloofness could have been one of the factors in his fight with Catherine's brother Arthur.

Being an only child (other than his three half siblings with whom he lived perhaps a year) almost certainly contributed to Newton's isolation, but this wasn't the primary reason he sought privacy. As Catherine said, Newton spoke little and thought much, and the quiet allowed him to think. As one biographer put it, "Solitude was the essential part of his genius."[10] Even if it was initially his seclusion that forced Newton's thoughts to become his main source of friendship, he would later voluntarily seek out seclusion to spend more time with these private friends. This became a lifelong habit—seclusion and contemplation—and Newton fiercely guarded his privacy. Solitude enabled him to focus his mental and physical energy in ways that ordinary people simply cannot, given the multitude of things vying for their attention.

But at first, it seems that privacy was more a source of loneliness and pain, even if it allowed him to "play philosophically" (science was his play), as one early biographer put it.[11] We can't be sure, but there are English phrases in one of Newton's first notebooks that indicate his unhappiness. The phrases were to be translated into Latin as an exercise, but their nature is difficult to ignore: "A little fellow." "Hee is paile; There is no room for me to sit; In the top of the house—In the bottom of hell." "What imployment is he fit for? What is he good for?" "I will make an end. I cannot but weepe. I know not what to doe."[12] If autobiographical, then we see that Newton's isolation mostly affected him negatively, despite some of its eventual advantages.

Newton was an adept craftsman, even in his youth, possessing skills that laid the foundation for his famous scientific discoveries. According to his earliest biographer, William Stukeley, Granthamites knew young Newton for

> his strange inventions, uncommon skill & industry in mechanical works. they tell us, that insted of playing among the other boys, when from school, he always busyed himself at home, in making knicknacks of divers sorts, & models in wood, of whatever his fancy led him to. For which purpose he furnished himself with little saws, hatchets, hammers, chizels, & a whole shop of tools; which he would use with as much dexterity, as if he had been brought up to the trade, & all the money, his mother gave him, went in the purchase of 'em.[13]

This was what it meant to "play philosophically."

Newton copied many of his models from books, particularly *The Mysteries of Nature and Art* by John Bate and *Mathematical Magick* by John Wilkins (Wilkins would become one of the Royal Society's founders). During this period we already see Newton taking pages of notes from these books and whatever else he read. This is a habit he kept the rest of his life. Merely reading wasn't enough; he wanted to *keep* the treasures he found. To help his memory, he would sometimes copy passages from books repeatedly. The notebooks Newton accumulated over his life give us an idea of what sorts of things interested him. From Bates's book, for example, Newton copied down directions on drawing, catching birds (by making them drunk), making fish bait, mixing paints (Newton was fascinated with colors), and making cures for sicknesses. One cure is particularly enticing: "drinking twice or thrice a day a . . . small portion of mint & wormwood & 300 Millipedes well beaten (when their heads are pulled off) in a mortar . . . & suspended in 4 gallons of Ale in its fermentation."[14] The active ingredient was no doubt the last one.

Newton's notebooks also reveal an almost obsessive organizing tendency. Rather than merely copying random bits, Newton would organize and systematize them under general headings. He organized everything—from theology to natural philosophy (what we call "science") to language itself. (In one of his early notebooks he organized 2,400 nouns, taking up forty-two pages.) Newton could not look at the world without trying to make it fit together into a coherent whole. This would be another key to his discoveries.

Chief among Newton's little creations were clocks and sundials. He was fascinated with time, and the motion of the sun, planets, and stars on which time was based. Sometimes he built sundials in the rooms of Clark's house. It's surprising that Clark tolerated this since these dials consisted of wooden pegs hammered into the walls. Newton also built sundials into the wall at Woolsthorpe manor, and even built one at the Colsterworth church—when he was only nine. Newton's sundials were uncommonly accurate, measuring time down to a quarter of an hour, and Clark's family and neighbors would all consult what became known as "Isaac's dials."[15] Newton studied the dials so carefully that he could calculate the equinoxes and solstices, as well as the day of the month. Even later in life he would tell time in his house by glancing at the shadows on the walls rather than by looking at a clock, since, for him, shadows were just as accurate. At least during the day.

Wind was another theme in Newton's "philosophical" amusements. He would make his own kites, constantly improving their designs, carefully adjusting the shape, size, and location of the strings. Once he attached a homemade paper lantern to the end of a kite, causing a stir among the locals, who mistook it for an omen-bearing comet. He also patiently watched workmen build a windmill in Grantham, eventually making his own small replica that went beyond the capabilities of the original. He even fitted the mill with a device that allowed a mouse—which he called his "miller"—to turn the mechanism.

Newton spent hours in Clark's apothecary shop, where he learned to mix ointments and other medicines, becoming familiar with the properties of plants, minerals, and metals. This no doubt contributed to his interest in what we now call chemistry (or even alchemy, which had yet to be separated from chemistry). His interest in chemistry would consume more of his time than physics and mathematics put together; the only other subjects that occupied him more were theology and biblical studies. Newton's time at the apothecary's shop surely contributed to his lifelong habit of treating his own illnesses, which, given the state of medicine, no doubt contributed to his long life. Only when he became seriously ill in his eighties did he call for a doctor.

Newton also liked to draw and was fairly good at it. He left charcoal drawings and etchings on his walls in Clark's attic (Clark was obviously long-suffering)—pictures of plants, ships, portraits, animals, and birds. In the twentieth century, renovators at Woolsthorpe manor found Newton's geometric drawings in the walls. And everywhere we find "I. Newton" etched in wood.

All of this—his craftsmanship, artistic abilities, attention to detail, patience, and skills of observation—contributed to his later scientific success. Stukeley recognized that

> Sir Isaac's early use, & expertness at his mechanical tools, & his faculty of drawing, & designing, were of service to him, in his experimental way of philosophy: & prepar'd for him, a solid foundation to exercise his strong reasoning facultys upon; his sagacious discernment of causes, and effects, his most penetrating investigation of methods to come at his intended purpose; his profound judgment; his invincible constancy, & perseverance in finding out his solutions, & demonstrations, & in his experiments; his vast strength of mind, in protracting his reasonings, his chain of deductions; his indefatigable attachment to calculations; his incomparable skill in algebraic, & the like methods of notation; all these united in one man, & that in an extraordinary degree, were the architects that raisd a building upon the experimental foundation, which must stand coeval with material creation.[16]

Newton became one of the greatest experimenters in history. He could make measurements with such precision that they far outstripped those of his contemporaries, to the point that a few natural philosophers accused him of fabricating his results, an accusation that especially irked him.

But Newton could get carried away by his obsession with building, reading, and experimenting. He would sometimes neglect his schoolwork, which then forced him to work furiously to catch up. Nevertheless, he excelled at his studies, at least after Arthur Storer's vanquishing.

The school at Grantham, the highly reputable School of King Edward VI (or, The King's School), was more than three hundred years old and provided the standard classical education based on Latin and the Bible. The curriculum at Grantham also included Greek and Hebrew, but only a smattering of mathematics. The headmaster, Henry Stokes, was a devoted and well-respected educator. We know him, however, as the man who "discovered" Newton. He was responsible for encouraging Hannah to allow Isaac to prepare for the university rather than become a farmer.

King's School also had a Puritan bent, and one of its lecturers, John Angell, was a Puritan theologian who probably helped Newton along the strong religious path he walked the rest of his life. But the Puritanism of Newton's religion wasn't the caricature of Puritans with which we're familiar. For Puritans—and for Newton—earthly pleasures were gifts from God, if not taken to excess. We know, for example, Newton drank a pint now and then.

Rather, Newton's Puritanism placed an emphasis on personal holiness and the authority of Scripture. For Newton, holiness included industriousness, self-discipline, and the constant guarding against the vanity of pride. But more than that, his religion was personal, a relationship with God. Newton's God was not the aloof or even impersonal God of the philosophers. Newton recognized that God was his Father, which was something he was born without. Many of Newton's biographers have inferred from his posthumous status a resulting lifelong desire to please his heavenly Father.

But Newton was also Anglican, and this manifested itself mostly in his respect for the Church Fathers. As he did with most things he studied, he mastered their writings, comparing their consistency with Scripture. But since Scripture's authority trumped the Fathers', Newton would disagree with the Fathers if ever he felt they differed from the Bible. Ironically, Newton's unswerving adherence to Scripture's authority would lead him to disagree with certain aspects of the doctrine of the Trinity.

Headmaster Stokes recognized Newton's academic potential and encouraged him in his studies, gently admonishing him for spending too much time building or in extracurricular reading. And although Newton wouldn't entirely lay aside his extracurricular pursuits, he found that studying was what he was built for; he had finally found his niche. If there was one thing he excelled at, it was learning.

But after four and a half years at Grantham, when Newton was almost seventeen, his mother called him home to Woolsthorpe midyear. She wanted him to follow his father's footsteps as a gentleman farmer.

2

A NARROW ESCAPE

Isaac's return to Woolsthorpe must have disappointed and frustrated him. If he had begun to dream of his future as a scholar—a dream in which Stokes no doubt encouraged him—he was now waking up from that dream.

We don't know whether, to show his displeasure, Newton intentionally made life difficult for his mother and the servants at Woolsthorpe, but if so, he was wildly successful. His passive aggression—if that is what it was—has become famous. During times when he should have been tending the sheep, he would be lost in a book while the flock wandered the countryside. Or instead of mending fences, he would make water wheels in the streams. The manor court at Colsterworth fined Newton for allowing sheep or pigs to roam freely in neighboring fields and for letting his fences fall into disrepair.

Newton was the picture of an absentminded bookworm. Sometimes he would get so completely absorbed in his own thoughts, or in a book, that he would forget to eat. At Cambridge, he would become famous for missing meals. Once, while casually leading his horse up a hill by its bridle, he was so engaged in a book that when the horse slipped out of its bridle, Newton failed to notice, walking miles before realizing it. Meanwhile, the horse reached home safely.

Hannah finally assigned a servant to shadow Newton, to ensure that he behaved and to teach him how to run an estate. This didn't go nearly as well as Hannah planned. When it was time to travel into Grantham for supplies and to sell goods, Newton would bribe the servant to let him sneak away after they got around the first corner in the road. Newton would then read or build things until the servant came back at the end of the day. Other times, Newton made it all the way to Grantham with the servant, but would then head straight to the apothecary's house to read the books stored in the attic.

On one occasion, Newton's uncle William Ayscough (Hannah's brother) found the young farmer doing mathematics under a hedge instead of doing his chores. This was probably not a surprise to Ayscough, given Newton's record. William—taking advantage of the incident—suggested that Hannah allow Isaac to return to Grantham "to prepare for the university."[1]

Stokes, too, urged Hannah "not to bury such hopeful talents,"[2] presumably referring to academic and not agricultural talent. He promised Hannah that Newton would become a great man and even waived the additional "out of state" tuition that King's School charged anyone living more than a mile away. He also offered to have Newton board at his own house. (Perhaps Joseph Clark had had enough of Newton's remodeling.)

But it was a difficult sell to Hannah. She had lost two husbands and now had a farm that needed oversight. Furthermore, she had long cultivated Newton's prospects as a future yeo-man, prospects much more realistic than those promised by Stokes and Ayscough. But given Stokes's persistence and her brother's advice, Hannah finally conceded, allowing Newton to return to Grantham in 1660, after serving nine months' time at Woolsthorpe. The servants at Woolsthorpe apparently agreed that Hannah made the right decision: they "rejoic'd at parting with him, declaring, he was fit for nothing but the 'Versity."[3] As David Berlinski writes, it was "a narrow escape from the plow."[4]

Newton's mentors, Ayscough and Stokes, had already decided that Newton should attend Trinity College at Cambridge—no surprise, given that both had attended Cambridge themselves. Furthermore, Humphrey Babington, Mrs. Clark's brother, was senior fellow at Trinity. But before Newton could leave for Cambridge, he still had nine months of high school waiting for him in Grantham. So he bought a Greek lexicon and a commentary on the New Testament and returned with Stokes to King's School. Catherine Storer was probably just as delighted as Isaac for his return to Grantham.

Newton's remaining time at Grantham was uneventful, and nine months later, when it was time for Newton to graduate and depart for Cambridge, Stokes had Newton stand in front of the class. He gave Newton a rousing farewell speech and admonished the others to follow his example. Stukeley reported that not only did Stokes get misty eyed, but that some of the boys also came to tears. If that is true, then the boys' estimation of Newton had changed dramatically.

Although Stokes died before Newton published his greatest

works, his prophesy was entirely accurate—Newton became a great man.

In June 1661, when Newton was eighteen, he arrived by carriage at the White Lion Inn in Cambridge, after traveling three days from Woolsthorpe. The following day he made his way to Cambridge University's leading college, Trinity College. Cambridge University was more than four hundred years old and now the heart of English Puritanism. Former Oxford University scholars had founded it in the 1200s after a conflict with the Oxford locals, or townies. Cambridge would also be the place of Newton's second births—of both his genius and maybe even his soul, although such things are often difficult to judge. And though Newton had escaped the plow, he still had to labor physically for his freedom. He entered Trinity College as a subsizar, a class of student occupying the lowest social caste at Cambridge. Subsizars—and sizars, which Newton quickly became—had to earn their living and education by working as servants for professors or wealthy students. Newton made his way by cleaning boots, dressing hair, or emptying chamber pots.

It wasn't nearly as bad as it could have been. Newton was sizar to Catherine's uncle, Humphrey Babington, a fellow of Trinity. Babington was only in Cambridge a few months out of the year, leaving Newton with the freedom that other sizars could only envy.

Taking into account his mother's wealth, it is puzzling that Newton should have had to put himself through college this way. We know that Hannah was annoyed by Newton's "bookishness,"[5] so perhaps Hannah thought the hard work would be good for Newton, that getting his head out of a book once in a while would make him appreciate the luxury of learning. She may have also been a penny-pincher—one of the ways Stokes had convinced her to allow Newton's return to Grantham was by remitting the forty-shilling fee for students from outside Grantham.

Newton himself was apparently thrifty (good thing, too, for later in life he would find himself in charge of the London Mint). He made scrupulous records of his finances, which give us further insight into his day-to-day life. When he first arrived at college, he bought the following necessities: an ink bottle and ink, a notebook with 140 blank pages, candles—lots of candles—and a lock for his desk. (And of course, a chamber pot, which he emptied himself.) Later he purchased a chess set and a membership to the tennis courts—the latter he never used.

But despite his frugalness, he was also generous with his money. He would loan money to other students, even wealthier students. Most paid him back.

In the 1300s the Cambridge curriculum turned decidedly Aristotelian—with Aristotelianism's earth at the center of the cosmos, its division of the physical universe into heavenly and earthly realms, and its speculations about why objects fall to the ground (objects *want* to) and why a thrown ball keeps moving after it leaves your hand (you've imparted to the ball an *impetus* that it gradually uses up, falling to the earth). Cambridge was still on the Aristotelian course when Newton arrived in the 1660s. Although we have to piece together Newton's studies from his notebooks, we can be sure that the official curriculum was largely a course in the Scholastic worldview—a worldview that wedded Christianity with Aristotelianism. But the Aristotelian half—certainly not Scholasticism's better half—was being challenged outside Cambridge. Aristotle's reign was under attack. Newton would soon discover this, but in the meantime, he set himself to learning Aristotle with characteristic intensity.

During his first year or two at Cambridge, Newton studied Aristotle's logic, ethics, physics, and metaphysics. And given Newton's love of systematizing, his first encounters with Aristotle's vast and intricate system must have been a heady experience. One thing Newton held in common with Aristotle was the desire to piece together *everything*. Understanding—as opposed to merely being informed—requires that subjects be seen in the context of a bigger picture, how they all fit together. Throughout his life, Newton devoted tremendous energy to constructing a coherent story of reality—fitting together history, physics, mathematics, chemistry, and theology. Ironically, Newton's work would complete Aristotle's overthrow in European universities. One systematizer replacing another.

Cambridge assigned all incoming students a tutor—someone to oversee their education as well as be their primary lecturer. The quality of a student's education, therefore, largely depended upon the tutor. Newton's tutor, Benjamin Pulleyn, was a professor of Greek and left Newton almost entirely alone. This isn't surprising: Pulleyn had a reputation for being a "pupil monger," a tutor who would take on additional students in order to augment his income. Pulleyn had dozens of students, most of whom probably received from him the same education he gave to Newton.

For Newton, however, Pulleyn's "teaching" style was a blessing. Newton was a first-rate autodidact; from childhood, he excelled at teaching and learning, singly playing both roles at once. His university-sanctioned tutor, therefore, allowed him the freedom to continue what he had done for years: read *whatever* he wanted, *whenever* he wanted. And for now, he wanted to explore Aristotelianism. (We know of two times when Newton attended Pulleyn's lectures—one on Sanderson's *Logic* and another on Kepler's *Optics*. In both cases, Newton showed up knowing more than his tutor.)

At Cambridge he continued his habit of taking extensive reading notes in a commonplace notebook. He started each new notebook at the front and back simultaneously, working inward toward the center. While an undergraduate, Newton consciously modified his handwriting from his more elaborate youthful script, to a quicker, more efficient form. But he always wrote very neatly and very small, wasting precious little paper.

One of Newton's two main notebooks from his under-graduate years at Cambridge provides the first real insight into his religious life. In 1662, at Pentecost of his freshman year, Newton listed fifty-eight sins. We aren't sure what prompted this confession; some biographers think that it was in response to an inner crisis. Perhaps it was the occasion of his conversion, or at least of his "owning his faith." We simply don't know.

Many of the sins on Newton's list deal with Sabbath-breaking: "Eating an apple at Thy house . . . Making a mousetrap on Thy day . . . Squirting water on Thy day . . . Missing cha-pel . . . Carelessly hearing and committing many sermons." Others signify that Newton was aware of his heart's inclination to turn away from God: "Setting my heart on money learning pleasure more than Thee . . . Not turning nearer to Thee for my affections . . . Not living according to my belief . . . Not loving Thee for Thy self . . . Not desiring Thy ordinances . . . Neglecting to pray . . . Fearing man above Thee." He also repented of sins toward his family and others: "Denying a crossbow to my mother and grandmother though I knew of it . . . Punching my sister . . . Peevishness with my mother . . . With my sister."[6] He even asked God to forgive him for his pivotal fight with Arthur Storer.

But there are two disturbing confessions: "Threatning my father and mother Smith to burne them and the house over them" and "Wishing death and hoping it to some."[7] The first occurred before Newton was eleven, but both sins reveal an anger that, if unchecked, could quickly get away from him. He would work his entire life at mortifying his temper.

Newton always said that one of the ways he resisted sexual temptation was by diverting his attention with intense study and contemplation, advice that he gave to others. Freudians and other sensationalists have a great time with this, suggesting that it was really sexual frustration that drove Newton. It's an entertaining theory, but it suffers from one troublesome fault: there's little to support it.

Speaking of entertainment, many of Newton's fellow students—like students of today—took advantage of their new independence by frequenting taverns and houses of ill repute. This had become such a serious problem that Cambridge legislated punishment as an attempt to curb the promiscuity. And when the yearly Sturbridge Fair arrived—the largest fair in England and the one after which Bunyan modeled Vanity Fair—entertainment could get out of hand.

Newton's first roommate must have been intent on taking

every advantage of his college experience. But for Newton—
who grew up an only child, who was trying to live a Christian life,
and who was intent on spending time alone with his thoughts—a
raucous roommate was too much to bear. (No doubt his roommate had trouble bearing with Newton. Newton was known to
reprimand anyone who spoke of religion lightly in his presence;
and once, his niece conveyed, he "got on well" with Joahn Francis
Vigani, a "chymistry" professor at Trinity, until Vigani "told
a loose story about a nun."[8]) In his sophomore year, Newton
met the "Bible-loving John Wickins,"[9] another student who was
dealing with "disorderly companions." Years later, just before
Newton's death in 1727, Wickins' son, Nicholas, recalled:

> My Father's Intimacy with Him came by meer Accident. My
> Fathers first Chamber-fellow being very disagreeable to him
> he retired one day into the walks, where he found Mr Newton
> solitary & dejected; Upon entering into discourse they found
> their cause of Retirement the same, & thereupon agreed to
> shake off their present disorderly Companions & Chum [or
> room] together, which they did as soon as conveniently they
> could & so continued as long as My Father staid at College.[10]

Wickins and Newton were well suited for one another: they
roomed together for twenty years. Later, Newton would also
employ Wickins as his amanuensis—his secretary and copyist.

With his living situation greatly improved, Newton was now
able to focus more on his studies. For his first eighteen months
or so at Cambridge, Newton studied the standard Scholastic
curriculum. Aristotle's views—combined with Christian

theology—had held sway for centuries, and these views fed Newton's sprawling imagination. As he sprawled, however, he encountered contemporary works in natural philosophy, works attacking Aristotle's musty reign. A revolution was taking place, a scientific revolution—*the* scientific revolution. And although Newton undoubtedly felt a special kinship with Aristotle's all-encompassing systematizing, and with Aristotle's attempt to build a single, coherent worldview, Newton would soon become the coup's leader. But before commanding the revolutionaries, he must sit at their feet and learn.

(3)

AT THE FEET OF GIANTS

In a 1676 letter to Robert Hooke, the Royal Society's curator of experiments, Newton wrote that, if he had seen further than most men, it was only because he had stood on the shoulders of giants. Newton had no delusions of grandeur; he was well aware that he built his innovations upon the work of others.

Although Aristotle is one of the giants on whose shoulders Newton—and just about everyone else—would stand, Newton suddenly stopped taking notes on Aristotle midway through the Cambridge curriculum. Passages from more contemporary authors began showing up in his commonplace book. These contemporaries were pretenders to Aristotle's throne, and Newton was intrigued.

The university hadn't meant to expose Newton to revolutionary ideas. Yet the freedom Newton had been given under the "tutelage" of Pulleyn allowed him to set aside the university-sanctioned course of study and venture out into the contemporary world of scholarship. He was almost completely on his own, as he preferred it, and consumed the revolutionary ideas at an alarming rate.

The Polish astronomer Nicolaus Copernicus sparked the scientific revolution. A century before Newton, Copernicus had thrown a boulder into the quiet, stagnant pond of European science. He claimed that the sun—*not* the earth—was at the center of the universe. And amazingly he had no new observations to back up his claim; heliocentrism just made the math simpler. It is one of the great mysteries in science that anyone would reason from simplicity to truth. Yet we do it today and no one really knows why.

The revolution intensified when the German mathematician and astronomer Johannes Kepler (he was also an astrologer) discovered that the orbits of the planets were ellipses, not circles. And yet again, this was a case of simpler mathematics; Kepler used no new substantive observations. By 1619, he had published all three of his laws of planetary motion. They were not, however, *laws* when Newton was an undergraduate but merely alternative ways of accounting for the astronomical data. Newton's later work would turn them into legislation.

Another anti-Aristotelian conspirator was the Italian physicist and astronomer Galileo Galilei, who died the year Newton was born, 1642. In 1609, Galileo had used observations made with his homemade refracting telescope to argue that the sun, moon, planets, and stars were—contrary to Aristotle—made from earth, air, fire, and water, rather than from a special fifth element, or quintessence. The moon had pockmarks, and the sun had spots that continually changed. Apparently, then, there weren't two separate realms—"earthly" and "heavenly"—but merely one, composed of a single type of matter. If this is true, Galileo said, then nature is uniform, and it would be theoretically possible to formulate a single set of laws to describe terrestrial *and* celestial phenomena. This, Newton would do.

Galileo also campaigned to include experiments and mathematics in natural philosophy. To us, this is entirely obvious, but only because we stand downstream of the revolution. Aristotle's scientific method was primarily speculative, based on minimal observation and no experimentation or mathematics to speak of. Furthermore, Aristotle's physics was qualitative and not quantitative. Aristotelians expressed their physical theories in terms of qualities like *lighter* and *heavier*, *faster* and *slower*, with no numbers attached to these qualities. But until speed, for example, could be quantified, natural philosophy would be hobbled.

This notion of *mathematically* describing physical phenomena or appearances wasn't new to Galileo, but it had been neglected. The dream of mathematical descriptions of the cosmos began in ancient Greece. Plato—Aristotle's teacher—set "mathematizing" nature as the goal of his Academy in Athens. He called it "saving the phenomena." But this was just too difficult without the proper tools, without the proper mathematics. It was left to Newton to take Plato's idea to fruition, making it standard operating procedure for modern science.

The man who had the most significant influence on Newton during these undergraduate years was the French philosopher and mathematician René Descartes, who died in 1650, when Newton was eight. Descartes felt that the Aristotelian-centered curriculum was nearly bankrupt and made a conscious effort to replace Scholasticism in Europe's educational centers with his own philosophical system.

The difference between Descartes' universe and Aristotle's is best described with metaphors. Aristotle's cosmos was like a biological organism, Descartes' like a clock. In Aristotle's world, rocks fell to the earth because that was their nature—they desired to reach their natural place of rest. In Descartes' universe, however, matter is entirely inert. There is no *built-in* desire or plan. All motion is caused by matter bumping into matter, always by physical contact, like billiard balls. In the case of falling rocks, Descartes explained that the rocks are pushed toward the earth by particles of invisible matter, called ether.

Because motion was caused only by matter coming into contact with other matter, the planets, too, must be moved by some material stuff. Again, Descartes brought ether in to play this role. Rather than a vacuum existing throughout space, space was occupied by this ethereal, imperceptible fluid. The sun pushed the ether around, forming swirling vortices like whirlpools directly downstream of rocks. These vortices of ether in turn pushed the planets around the solar system, not unlike little ships in a complex system of whirlpools.

Newton would sign on to the Cartesian mechanical philosophy (the name given to the philosophical doctrine of René Descartes), only later abandoning some of its central tenets—including ether and vortices. Ironically, it is Newton—and not Descartes—who is famous for our clocklike view of the universe.

Since clocks are much simpler than organisms, a mechanical view of the universe was more optimistic, more accessible.

It was kinder and gentler in terms of relinquishing its secrets to mortals. And it is much easier to describe mathematically, which was Descartes' ultimate goal. And so Descartes invented a new tool to assist him in his mathematization of the world: analytic geometry, which employs Cartesian coordinates, so named after its inventor. Without analytic geometry, modern science would not exist; nor would Newton's calculus.

Such was the state of the scientific revolution at the time Newton set aside Cambridge's official curriculum. Natural philosophers were mathematizing, mechanizing, and unifying. The troops were advancing and had just recruited a young Cambridge student who, when the dust of the coup settled, would occupy Aristotle's throne. But the current ideas were not yet sufficient to completely overthrow Aristotle; even more radical ideas were needed. Once Newton learned from Copernicus, Kepler, Galileo, and Descartes, he began to arrive at ideas even more revolutionary.

4

"CERTAIN PHILOSOPHICAL QUESTIONS"

After Newton stopped taking notes on Aristotle, there were still a hundred blank pages in the middle of his notebook. It is in this part of the notebook that Newton took notes on the authors of the new mechanical philosophy. But he quickly advanced to commenting on their ideas, criticizing them, and arriving at new ideas. He began this new stage of study by asking questions of the contemporary authors. At the top of the empty section's first page, he wrote "Quaestiones quaedam Philosophicae," or "Certain Philosophical Questions." He was respectful of these philosophers' authority but was also willing to venture out on his own, allowing questions to lead to innovative answers. Above the section's title, Newton wrote *Amicus Plato amicus Aristoteles magis amica veritas*: "Plato is my friend and Aristotle is my friend but my greater friend is truth."[1] With these philosophical questions, Newton began to climb toward the shoulders of giants.

One of the ways teachers determine how well their students understand new material is by the quality of their questions. Knowing what questions to ask—where the "sweet spot" of an issue is—is something that requires effort, insight, and intellectual horsepower. After reading Aristotle, Newton knew where the sweet spots were—he knew what questions to ask. He knew the intellectual terrain and set up his course of study accordingly.

Newton's agenda reveals his obsession with intellectual orderliness. In the "Quaestiones," he set out forty-five topics of study, beginning with the building blocks of the universe: *Of the First Matter*. From the outset, the Aristotelian influence is apparent—"first matter" or "prime matter" was an important Aristotelian term. Other topics of study include *Of Atoms, Quantity, Place, Time, Gravity & Levity, Colours, Sounds, Atraction Magneticall, Of Water & Salt flux & reflux of the Sea.*

Under the heading *Of God*, Newton wrote: "Were men & beasts &c made by fortuitous jumblings of attomes there would be many parts uselesse in them here a lumpe of flesh there a member too much some kinds of beasts might have had but one eye some more than two & the two eyes."[2] Underlying this simple and reasonable statement is something profound, something that underwrites Newton's entire natural philosophy. As Gale Christianson points out, "This was more than a passing observation; it was a reminder to himself that the underlying unity in nature, revealed to man through rational inquiry and observation is a product of the Divine Mind."[3] The notion of design is a theme that runs through Newton's work, one that would become more pronounced as he developed his natural philosophy.

The first two headings, *Of the First Matter* and *Of Atoms*, are notable for their position within the "Quaestiones." Although Newton's published writings on natural philosophy focus primarily on mechanics and optics, he wrote far more on the fundamental nature of matter. It is probably no coincidence that these two headings receive pride of place. His interest in chemistry—or what was called "chymistry" and sometimes even "alchemy"—would find greater manifestation over his life, and occupy more of his time than physics ever did. Only his biblical and theological studies attracted his attention more.

Newton had always been fascinated with light and colors. The ancient Greeks had systematically studied light, usually as a geometrical pursuit, but light's nature was still unknown during Newton's time—just as it is today. During his undergraduate years, Newton began performing experiments in optics. He even learned how to grind his own lenses. Some of his optical experiments from this time reveal Newton's determination to unlock the mysteries of light. Newton performed some of the optical experiments on human eyes—his own.

Under the heading *On Imagination*, Newton recounted staring at the reflection of the sun to determine its effects on his eyes. After repeating the experiment a few times, he was essentially blind, seeing nothing but the after-image of the sun. He recalled to John Locke how his eyesight finally returned:

I durst neither write nor read: but to recover the use of my eyes, shut myself up in my chamber made dark, for three days together, and used all means to divert my imagination from the sun. For if I thought upon him, I presently saw his picture, though I was in the dark. But by keeping in the dark, and employing my mind about other things, I began in three or four days to have some use of my eyes again; and by forbearing a few days longer to look upon bright objects, recovered them pretty well, though not so well, but that for some months after the spectrum of the sun began to return as often as I began to meditate upon the phenomenon, even though I lay in bed at midnight with my curtains drawn; but now I have been very well for many years, though I am apt to think, that if I durst venture my eyes, I could still make the phantasm return by the power of my fancy.[4]

If that weren't enough, about a year later Newton performed another dangerous experiment in which he took a bodkin (a dull needlelike piece of metal) and stuck it "betwixt my eye & the bone as near to the backside of my eye as I could."[5] We can be confident that Newton never uttered the motto "Safety first" and we see how far he was willing to go to meet his friend truth.

Sometime in 1663, when Newton was a junior, he visited the Sturbridge Fair. Located along the River Cam, the fair was essentially a huge market. In addition to a low-quality prism, Newton purchased a book on astrology. He was befuddled by a diagram of constellations, which required trigonometry to understand. So he began to teach himself trigonometry. He in turn discovered that, in order to understand trigonometry, he needed geometry, so he began studying Euclid's *Elements*. His response to Euclid was apparently designed to please future geometry students: he looked at a number of the propositions and thought it an entire waste of time to prove truths that are so obvious. So Newton discarded the most important mathematical text in history, out of hand.

Time, however, changed his estimation of Euclid, and he eventually regretted taking the *Elements* so lightly. In fact, a famous anecdote about Newton is told against the backdrop of his high esteem of Euclid's geometry. Humphrey Newton (no relation), Newton's roommate and amanuensis for five years in the 1680s, said that he could only remember Newton laughing once. In a letter to John Conduit, he wrote:

> His carriage then was very meek, sedate & humble, never seemingly angry, of profound Thoughts, his Countenance mild, pleasant & Comely; I cannot say, I ever saw him laugh, but once, which was at that Passage, which Dr. Stewkley mentioned in his Letter, to your Honour which put me in mind of the Ephesian Phylosopher, who laugh'd only once in his Life Time, to see an Ass, eating Thistles, when Plenty of Grass was by.[6]

The report of William Stukeley (the "Stewkley," to which Humphrey referred) elaborated on the occasion of Newton's laugh:

> he askd a friend to whom he had lent an Euclid to read, what progress he had made in that author? & how he liked it? he answerd by desiring to know what use, & benefit in life, that kind of study would be to him? upon which Sir Isaac was very merry.[7]

This story is very similar to an ancient tale in which Euclid himself was asked by a student whether geometry is useful. In response Euclid sarcastically directed his servant to give the student a coin since, as Euclid quipped, "he must make gain out of what he learns."[8]

Stukeley's memory of Newton's solemn personality was a bit different from Humphrey's, for in the same letter he continued:

> according to my own observation, tho'. Sir Isaac was of a very serious, & compos'd frame of mind, yet I have often seen him laugh, & that upon moderate occasions. he had in his disposition, a natural pleasantness of temper, & much good nature, very distant from moroseness, attended neither with gayety nor levity. he usd a good many sayings, bordering on joke, and wit. in company he behavd very agreably; courteous, affable, he was easily made to smile, if not to laugh.[9]

Despite Newton's belated appreciation of Euclid's geometry, he set it aside as an undergraduate and immediately turned to Descartes' *Geometrie*, a much more difficult text. Newton read a few pages of the *Geometrie* and got immediately stuck. He returned to the beginning. The second time through, he progressed a page or two further before running into more difficulties. Again, he read from the beginning, this time getting further still. He continued this process until he mastered Descartes' text. Had Newton mastered Euclid first, Descartes' analytic geometry would have been much easier to understand. Newton later advised others to not make his same mistake.

But Descartes had ignited Newton's interest in mathematics,

an interest that bordered on obsession. For the next two years or so, Newton plunged himself into a private study of mathematics. In March of his junior year, 1664, Newton attended Isaac Barrow's inaugural Lucasian lectures on mathematics. Henry Lucas, a member of Parliament, endowed the Lucasian Chair of Mathematics in 1663 as a way to compete with Oxford University's earlier establishment of similar professorship. Barrow—one of the finest mathematicians in England—was the first to occupy the Lucasian Chair.

Only a decade or so earlier, Barrow had been a lowly sizar just entering Cambridge. Nevertheless, he excelled at just about every subject, mastering Greek, theology, medicine, church history, astronomy, and finally mathematics. Although Barrow's lectures may have encouraged Newton's interest in mathematics, there is no indication that Barrow taught Newton much on the subject. Newton's education was now entirely self-directed. Most students would flail helplessly in his position, reading here and there and going nowhere. Newton, however, was usually the best teacher for Newton, his temporary rejection of Euclid notwithstanding.

A month later, in April 1664, Newton came to a crossroads in his career, one at which Barrow stood. In order for students to continue at Cambridge, they had to undergo an exam qualifying them for the status of scholar—a scholarship. Not only did the scholarship enable the student to remain at Cambridge and become eligible to earn a degree, it also carried a small stipend, which Newton could certainly use. Barrow, who proctored the exam, unfortunately tested Newton on Euclid's *Elements*. Ironically, Newton was well versed in more advanced mathematics, including Descartes' *Geometrie*. But Newton didn't mention this to Barrow, and is so Barrow was astounded at Newton's lack of preparation in what was then—and is still—the most important mathematics text in history. It is, in fact, one of the most important books period.

Surprisingly, Newton passed his scholarship exam, gained permanency at Cambridge, and advanced beyond sizar. It's unclear how this happened. Perhaps Newton had astounded Barrow on some other text or even some other subject—both were interested in Scripture, theology, and church history. Or maybe, as the Newton scholar Richard Westfall suggested, Newton's reputation as a brilliant and highly motivated student preceded him. Students who have both an aptitude and desire for learning always delight teachers, for such students are tragically rare. But Westfall thought the most likely explanation for Newton's successful examination is that he had an advocate in Humphrey Babington, Catherine Storer's uncle. Babington was on the verge of becoming a senior fellow at Trinity and perhaps—just as Stokes and Ayscough had done earlier—exercised enough influence to save Newton from another confrontation with farming.

Ironically, Babington's help in this matter would have made marriage to Catherine nearly impossible. Being made a scholar, Newton would likely stay in academia. But if Newton was eventually elected a fellow, which was probably in his plans, he would most likely never wed. Fellows were almost always required to take holy orders in the Anglican church, and they could only marry if they resigned their fellowship. In any case, learning of Newton's plans, Catherine married a Grantham attorney, Francis Bakon. Uncle Humphrey performed the ceremony. But Newton never forgot Catherine, nor she him. A year before Newton died, William Stukeley told him of his own plans to move to Grantham. Newton asked him to look into whether a certain house could be purchased because "his old acquaintance"[10] Catherine had lived there. Newton is rarely portrayed as sentimental, but this story reveals that his affection for Catherine lasted his entire life.

The following December, during his senior year at Cambridge, Newton began intently observing a comet that appeared suddenly in the English sky. Comets were freaks of nature; they would appear unexpectedly, traveling in what looked to be straight lines, then disappearing, never to be seen again. They were irregular, not part of the immutable, perfect quintessence out of which the other heavenly bodies were supposedly made. And so comets were omens, bearers of ill tidings, and so caused fear and consternation.

But to natural philosophers, they were puzzles to be solved. Newton warmly welcomed the opportunity to solve the puzzle. He stayed up all night watching the comet. A second one appeared a week later, again robbing Newton of his sleep. After the second comet disappeared, he continued watching the sky until a third appeared in April 1665. The behavior of comets would be one of the more important puzzles in Newton's development of his physics. But this incident during his senior year gives insight into Newton's personality. As he would do later—and to a more extreme degree—Newton pushed himself physically as well as mentally, entering into a dangerous state of exhaustion. David Brewster remarked that his "health was impaired to such a degree . . . that from this illness 'he learnt to go to bed betimes.'"[11]

And maybe his illness did temper his careless neglect of personal health and safety. If so, there is little evidence of it: he was cavalier whenever a philosophical problem gripped him, which was often. He was always occupied. The only rest he would take when studying would be to change subjects and continue studying some more. John Conduitt, Newton's nephew by marriage, wrote:

> At the University he spent the greatest part of his time in his closet & when he was tired with his severer studies of Philosophy his only relief & amusement was going to some other study as History, Chronology Divinity Chymistry all which he examined & searched thoroughly as appears by the many papers he has left on those subject.[12]

Newton himself had written in the "Quaestiones" notebook, "too much study, (whence & from extreame passion cometh madnesse)."[13] It seems that this warning was taken lightly, for he tempted madness on several occasions.

In April 1665—the same month the third comet appeared—Newton was awarded his bachelor's degree. He continued to work on mathematics. By this time, he had discovered his binomial theorem; and in May, Newton was already beginning to form the ideas of his calculus—what he would call the method of "fluxions." He was twenty-two.

But this work could not continue at Cambridge. The plague was dangerously approaching. Apparently, the comets were right.

5

THE ANNUS MIRABILUS

In April 1665, the bubonic plague surfaced in London, and Samuel Pepys wrote in his diary, "Great fears of the Sickenesse here in the City, it being said that two or three houses are already shut up. God preserve us all."[1] The plague spread, of course, and in order to avoid it, so did the people.

By summer, it had "pleased Almighty God in his just severity to visit this towne of Cambridge with the plague of pestilence."[2] The university closed its doors and many students took to the country with their tutors to continue their education. But Newton was in no need of a tutor and in the middle of the summer returned to Woolsthorpe alone. He would remain at home until April 1667, aside from a brief return to Cambridge in 1666 from March to June. But while Newton reposed in the comfort and isolation of the country, horrors raged in the cities, especially London. By September 1665, eight thousand cramped Londoners were dying each week.

In September 1666, yet another disaster befell England's chief city: most of London burned to the ground. First the plague, then the Great Fire. London seemed to be under judgment. There was talk of Armageddon. The very year, 1666, contained the number of the beast. Strangely, and thankfully, the results of the fire were almost the exact opposite of those of the plague. The plague devastated life, leaving buildings entirely intact; the Great Fire, however, killed only six people.

There was, however, another casualty of the Great Fire: books. London was home to scores of bookshops, where scholars could find volumes of important works—ancient and contemporary. We have no idea what knowledge was lost. Although the Great Fire was not as rampant as the fires that consumed ancient Alexandria's scrolls, for those who value learning, the loss was tragic.

This period of Newton's exile from Cambridge—these plague years—has been called Newton's *annus mirabilis*, his year of wonders. During this time Newton accomplished more than most could accomplish in many lifetimes. But the phrase *annus mirabilis*, scholars have noted, is misleading. For one thing, the exile lasted nearly two years, not one. This problem was easily fixed with grammar: *anni mirabilis*, the wonder *years*. The second problem is that the use of *mirabilis* to describe these years suggests that Newton's work during the plague was the most significant of his life. But the *anni* are really a continuation of the feverish and systematic study Newton began earlier and would continue later. To be sure, these were miraculous years for Newton, but other years were too.

Despite scholars' misgivings, however, this period *does* stand out in certain ways—even among Newton's lifetime. It was at Woolsthorpe that Newton left his teachers far behind, becoming the world's leading authority in mathematics and optics. He also made the first major steps in what would become his theory of gravity and the "System of the World."

Newton must have seen his exile as an opportunity to be left even more alone. "Exile" would have been a sweet word in his ears, even if "plague" was not. And if Newton felt any reluctance or guilt about following his own curriculum while still under the roof of Cambridge, he would find relief in the country.

Unlike most college kids, Newton wouldn't spend his time catching up on sleep or making some extra spending money. He was in earnest—perhaps more so than at Cambridge. He turned his old room at the top of the stairs into a study, building shelves to hold the books he brought home. At Woolsthorpe, he also had access to his stepfather's library—two to three hundred books' worth. In Smith's library, he found an old notebook, most of the pages empty. Smith had evidently planned to take theological notes. There were headings of intended areas of study, perhaps reminding Newton of himself. But Newton's similarity to Smith ended there. His stepfather had quickly lost interest in the program, taking very few notes. So Newton, never one to waste paper, used the notebook for his own studies. He called it the "Waste Book" and got down to work.

Good metaphors can outstrip literal descriptions. By the seventeenth century, books had been around long enough to become an important metaphor in natural philosophy. In *The Advancement of Learning* (1605), Francis Bacon wrote that there are "laying before us two books or volumes to study, if we will be secured from error; first the scriptures, revealing the will of God; and then the creatures expressing his Power."[3]

According to the metaphor, God has written two books—Scripture and Nature—and He is glorified by the study of either one. This view, this "belief in the sacral nature of science,"[4] was prevalent among natural philosophers of the seventeenth century. As Frank Manuel, one of Newton's most important twentieth-century biographers, says:

> The traditional use of science as a form of praise to the Father assumed new dimensions under the tutelage of Robert Boyle and his fellow-members of the Royal Society, and among the immediate disciples of Isaac Newton. . . . In the *Christian Virtuoso*, demonstrating that experimental philosophy assisted a man to be a good Christian, Boyle assured readers that God required not a slight survey, but a diligent and skilful scrutiny of His works.[5]

Although Newton's intensity while pursuing his work ranges from humorous to alarming, it is put into a different light if we see it as a measure of his devotion to God. For Newton, "To be constantly engaged in studying and probing into God's actions was true worship."[6] This idea defined the seventeenth-century scientist, and in many cases, the scientists doubled as theologians.

Newton, it is fair to say, doubled as both. As mentioned in an earlier chapter, although he was not known as a theologian, he wrote far more words on theology than anything else. Manuel writes that Newton knew the Bible "as few theologians did, and he could string out citations like a concordance."[7] Newton devoted his life to studying God's Word and his world. The discoveries for which he's famous are in the realm of the latter, but these are motivated, underwritten, and informed by Newton's knowledge of the former.

If nature is a book that humans can read, then it must be written in a language humans have the capacity to understand. But whereas the language of God's Word is clear enough—Greek, Hebrew, and a bit of Aramaic—the language of God's world still needed deciphering.

Millennia before, Pythagoras and Plato had believed that the cosmos was fundamentally mathematical and was designed that way by a divine creator. It was Galileo, however, who updated this notion and couched it in the book metaphor, claiming that nature was written in the language of geometry, of *mathematics*. And like any book, Galileo said, unless we understand nature's language, our studies will be like wandering in a "dark labyrinth."[8] But Galileo had little idea of what was to come—or how right he was.

The problem was that there was no sufficient language for motion. Yet the phenomena natural philosophers care most about involve motion. They still couldn't precisely describe the movement of physical objects, especially when the object's velocity varied. To be sure, if given the right phenomena, natural philosophers could capture a moment in time—and sometimes not even this—yet determining how an object's motion *changed* was an altogether different story. It was as if they could take pictures, but couldn't make movies.

Imagine a movie of an object flying through the air—a cat, perhaps. The more frames per second we have, the more of the cat's moments we capture, the more data we have. But if we wanted information about the cat at a moment in between any two of the frames, we would be forced to guess or approximate based on the frames before and after the missing moment.

Now, the cat's flight is continuous—there are no gaps. If we are to capture *every* moment of the flight, we need an infinite number of frames, since there is an infinite number of moments during the cat's travels. To make matters worse, in between any two moments, there is *another* infinite number of moments. And between any two of *those* moments, there are infinitely more moments. And so on, world without end.

So the problem is the ordinary, gapless motion we see in the book of nature. Whether cats or planets or comets, all moving objects travel distances made up of uncountably many moments. And the objects usually change velocity and direction during these moments. The language of nature, therefore, must be able to describe *all* these moments in a rigorous way.

And so Newton invented the necessary language—the calculus. As with other problems that Newton attacked, this one succumbed to his immense powers of concentration. When wrestling with a problem, Newton would "keep the subject constantly before me and wait 'till the first dawnings open slowly, by little and little, into a full and clear light."[9] He rarely lost a fight.

Newton had already begun to develop the calculus as an undergraduate. He had learned the latest developments on infinite series, and in the beginning of 1665, while a senior, he surpassed that work with his general binomial theorem. By the November after his graduation, he had solved this problem, arriving at his "method of fluxions" or what we call "derivatives."

In May 1666, at Woolsthorpe, he "had entrance into the inverse method of fluxions,"[10] or "fluents" (what we call "integrals"). In October 1666, he consolidated some of his mathematical discoveries in an essay titled "To Resolve Problems by Motion." The title—and the terms "fluent" and "fluxion"—hint at the way Newton thought of points, curves, and areas. He imagined, for example, that a curve is created by a moving point, as if the point draws the curve. He resolved purely mathematical problems by thinking of mathematical objects—points and lines—in motion. The analogy between the theoretical and the physical was no accident. With his new tool, Newton would solve problems of physical motion—something real—in terms of mathematical motion—something purely imaginary. This is one of the mysteries of mathematics.

In Woolsthorpe, the calculus now existed in its essential form (although Newton would refine it over his lifetime). In total seclusion, Newton had become the world's greatest mathematician.

The notion of infinity, however, still bothered Newton. And it should have. The concept had caused headaches ever since the ancient Greek philosopher Zeno, using infinity, produced a really good argument for the conclusion that motion is impossible. Greek mathematicians, therefore, gave infinity a wide berth. In the calculus, infinity manifested itself in infinitesimals—infinitely small quantities that had no real size yet were not zero either. Shortly after Newton's death, the Irish bishop and philosopher George Berkeley published an insightfully scathing critique of the conceptual underpinnings of the calculus, centering on the incoherence of infinitesimals. It would be almost two centuries before mathematicians discovered how to eliminate the incoherence. Before that, they simply used it because it worked.

Newton wasn't, however, the only mathematician to develop calculus. A decade later, the German philosopher Gottfried Leibniz arrived at a method similar to Newton's. Near the end of their lives, a fierce rivalry erupted between them, both men claiming priority in the calculus's invention.

Newton accomplished almost all he wanted to in mathematics during the *anni mirabilis*. He would never again devote himself completely to mathematics; any future work would be of the mopping-up kind. When he was much older, he told William Whiston "that no old Men . . . love Mathematicks."[11] But Newton's current enthusiasm for the beauty of the tool was evident. He once calculated a logarithm to fifty-five decimal places and the area under a hyperbola to fifty-two decimal places. He later admitted that his enthusiasm for his new methods got the better of him.

Given Newton's monumental work in mathematics at Woolsthorpe, it's surprising he did anything else. Ordinary things, like meals and sleep, no doubt gave way; but not natural philosophy and not, especially, the topics of gravity and light. Unbelievably, Newton advanced these disciplines as well.

When most people think of Newton, they think of an apple, and they think of it falling on his head. Newton's apple is the most popular piece of scientific folklore in history; it even outranks Archimedes' mad, naked dash through the streets, yelling, "Eureka!" Later in life, Newton told Stukeley the story of the apple. Newton and Stukeley had retired for their after-dinner tea in the garden of Newton's home in Kensington, just outside London. Stukeley recounted that they sat "under the shade of some appletrees, only he and myself. Admidst other discourse, he told me, he was just in the same situation, as when formerly, the notion of gravitation came into his mind. It was occasion'd by the fall of an apple, as he sat in the contemplative mood."[12] So an apple did, indeed, fall, but not on his head. Voltaire, one of Newton's greatest admirers, heard the story and spread it far and wide. The tale soon became legend, and in the nineteenth century, David Brewster reported that he "saw the apple tree in 1814, and brought away a portion of one of its roots. The tree was so much decayed that it was taken down in 1820, and the wood of it carefully preserved."[13]

It was at Woolsthorpe, during the wonder years, that the apple struck Newton's imagination, if not his head. In the orchard, Newton began to think of the extent of gravity's influence. The apple is pulled toward the center of the earth and it does so at the sea as well as on top of a mountain. How far might that influence extend? Could it possibly extend "to the orb of the moon"?[14] Newton asked himself. Could that same force be what keeps the moon in her orbit?

It is only because Newton asked these questions that we think their answers are so obvious. As with most brilliant ideas with which we have become familiar, it is difficult to imagine the questions' newness, their strangeness. The apple falls toward the earth's center; the moon doesn't. On the face of things, the two phenomena appear almost entirely *unlike*. It would take a genius or a madman to arrive at the conclusion that the apple's motion is caused by the same thing that causes the moon's.

Furthermore, what, exactly, *does* keep the moon from falling toward the center of the earth? Newton answered this incorrectly during the wonder years. He believed that the gravitational force is counterbalanced by another force, the "centrifugal" or center-fleeing force (coined by Dutch natural philosopher Christian Huygens). That is, gravity keeps the moon from floating off into space, while the centrifugal force keeps the moon from crashing into the earth. But this is incorrect—centrifugal force is no force at all. There is no such thing in this case. There *is* no outward force acting on the moon. Rather than being in a state of equilibrium, the moon is constantly "falling" about the earth. Its orbit is the result of gravity continually pulling the moon off its "natural" course, a course that would result from the moon's inertia if it were unhindered. But this, Newton did not yet know.

Newton asked one last question about gravity: what is the difference between how hard gravity pulls on the apple and how hard it pulls on the moon? In other words, how does the strength of gravity vary with distance? Newton answered this question correctly. He calculated that the force of earth's gravity varies according to an *inverse square law*. More specifically, as the distance between an object and the earth's center increases, the pull of gravity on that object decreases as the square of the distance increases. To make this idea more concrete, recall that your weight is a measure of how much gravity is pulling you. Now imagine that you weigh one hundred pounds on the surface of the earth (at sea level, let's say). Imagine also that you travel away from the earth to a distance twice as far from the earth's center as you were before. Your new weight is a measure of gravity's pull on you at your new location out in space. To calculate your new weight, take the factor by which your distance increased—in this case, it increased by a factor of two. Now square this number to get four. Because the change in gravity's strength is described by an *inverse* law, you would then *divide* your original weight by four, ending up with twenty-five pounds as your new weight. As your distance from the earth increased by a factor of two, gravity's pull on you decreased by a factor of four.

Newton checked his inverse square law against the available physical data, which included an erroneous value for the radius of the earth. Because this value was slightly off, Newton's calculations didn't exactly match known data; in his words, he "found them answer pretty nearly."[15] But not nearly enough, and Newton, slightly discouraged, would have to wait for more accurate data to prove his inverse square law. Relying on the astronomical observations of others would frustrate Newton again, causing another major conflict. In any case, this near miss may be one of the reasons that Newton—upon his return to Cambridge in 1667—mostly set aside his work on motion. But he was far from finished; he would revisit it in earnest in 1679.

We've been speaking as if gravity is a *thing*. But this is misleading. Newton was always reluctant to speculate on what gravity *is* or what *causes* it. He remained content merely describing physical phenomena, rather than explaining it. To call gravity a force only moves the question a step back into the darkness. Newton was still struggling with the very concept of a force, and it's no wonder. We still don't know what a force *is*. Even today, Newtonian gravity is a mystery, a catchall for effects of which we simply don't know the cause. In fact, Einstein's theory of general relativity eliminates a gravitational force altogether. Rather, the phenomena we formerly believed to be caused by gravity are caused by the curvature of space. As with most, if not all, of the fundamental concepts of physics, one mystery has been traded for another. And this would not surprise Newton. Despite his belief that the universe was in many ways intelligible, he knew it could never be intellectually tamed.

It would be twenty more years before Newton developed his theory of universal gravitation. During his exile, he never wrote of gravity being *mutual* between two objects. He only spoke of an attraction *from* the earth *to* the moon or *from* the sun *to* the planets, never vice versa. Furthermore, as we saw, he still didn't have the right answer to why the moon wasn't pulled out of its orbit toward the earth's center. Nevertheless, Newton had laid the foundation for his theory with the inverse square law. But we can see that our common belief that an apple gave Newton immediate insight into a full-blown theory of gravity belongs to Newtonian mythology. It also fails to appreciate the complexity of the theory and the immense amount of work Newton poured into developing it.

In the seventeenth century, everyone knew that color was a phenomenon produced by light. How light actually produced color, no one knew. At Cambridge Newton was already performing experiments to answer this question. He was obviously serious about the subject, to the detriment of his eyesight. It's no surprise, therefore, that his interest in optics traveled with him to Woolsthorpe. Nor is it surprising that Newton was familiar with the leading optical research of Descartes, Robert Boyle, and

Newton's future nemesis, Robert Hooke. It *is* surprising, however, that Newton found any time at all for optics.

According to the ancient Aristotelian view of light, white light is pure and unadulterated. Colored light, on the other hand, is derivative, a modification of white light. Seventeenth-century mechanical philosophy followed Aristotle on this score. Newton, however, would argue the exact opposite: white light, rather than being pure, is a mixture of colors. Not only was this a bold view, it is also entirely at odds with common sense. Ask any child whether white can be made by using crayons of other colors.

Newton's method of research in optics was different from that of mathematics and planetary motion. Whereas Newton's mathematical work occurred entirely on paper, and for the most part so did his work on gravity, in optics he relied primarily on experiments. It is one thing to calculate, quite another to experiment. Usually a scientist who excels in one isn't as well skilled in the other. Not even Einstein. As usual, however, Newton was not usual. He combined his theoretical knowledge with craftsmanship and Job-like patience. His Grantham days suggested this, but his research in optics would prove it.

One of the seventeenth century's masterpieces on optics was Robert Hooke's *Micrographia* (1665), and Newton was familiar with it. The *Micrographia* was Hooke's report on observations he had made with a microscope. Hooke, too, was a superb experimentalist, and he emphasized the use of a special type of experiment, what he called an *experimentum crucis*, or crucial experiment. Hooke had adapted this notion from Francis Bacon's famous *instantia crucis* or crucial instance. A crucial experiment is one that proves—and proves clearly—one hypothesis over its competitors. Such an experiment provides direction at a fork in the conceptual road.

While at Woolsthorpe, Newton developed an *experimentum crucis* to prove that white light was a combination of colors. The experiment used simple prisms and sunlight. The concept was simple, but its execution required unheard-of precision. Although Newton would continue to hone the procedure over the years, he felt that his Woolsthorpe experiment showed beyond doubt that white light was impure. To Newton, it was no mere hypothesis and he would clash with Hooke over this point.

Newton would also disagree with Hooke on the structure of light. Rather than light being impulses or waves, as Hooke and nearly everyone else believed, Newton believed that light was made of particles or "corpuscles." He was aware, however, that in this case he had no *experimentum crucis* for his view, and so it was only a hypothesis. Both Hooke and Newton were wrong. Light has characteristics of a wave and a particle but is neither. Like most things, light's fundamental nature is still a mystery.

In April 1667, Cambridge was free of the plague, and Newton returned to pursue his MA. During his time away from the academy, he had become Europe's leading mathematician as well as its leading expert on optics, and he had laid the foundation for his revolutionary theory of gravity. Out in the country, in the mind of a twenty-four-year-old, the scientific revolution had advanced further in a few months than it had in a century. And no one knew about any of it.

6

EMERGING

When he returned to Trinity, Newton's way of life changed very little, save for a few things. For one, he upgraded his workshop at Cambridge. His expense accounts show that he purchased new tools such as "[d]rills, gravers, a hone, a hammer, and a mandrill,"[1] which he used to make more tools. He also bought polishing putty for lenses and mirrors, a magnet, compasses, and cloth for his bachelor's robe. That Newton's workshop/laboratory was located in the apartment he shared with Wickins suggests that Wickins was long-suffering indeed.

From his detailed budget, we also learn that Newton took advantage of the taverns on occasion, where his friends apparently took advantage of him at cards (twice). Presumably this never occurred at Woolsthorpe. Other items on his expense list: a Bible binding, oranges for his sister, and money lent to Wickins (twice). And of course, he bought books.

Newton was a scholar—a bachelor of arts—receiving a small stipend as well as a few perquisites. But in the fall, his status would change, for better or worse. He was to undergo four days of oral exams in the chapel. If he passed, the senior fellows of Trinity College would elect him as a minor fellow. As a minor fellow, Newton would become a permanent fixture of the college, barring something serious, like being convicted of crime or heresy. Minor fellows were guaranteed a life of academic pursuits, for it was only a matter of time—a mere formality—before they would receive their master of arts and, in the same stroke, become a major fellow of the college. If Newton failed the exam, however, he would rejoin his mother at Woolsthorpe, not as a scholar on sabbatical as he had recently done, but as a shepherd.

The stakes were high, and the result of the exam wasn't a foregone conclusion. If the senior fellows questioned him on Cambridge's standard curriculum, then Newton might face difficulties—he had abandoned that course long ago.

He passed nonetheless. We don't know how. Maybe the senior fellows had gotten word of Newton's genius. Or maybe only Barrow examined him—and only on natural philosophy and mathematics, subjects Newton knew better than anyone. Whatever the case, on October 2, 1667, the fellows of Trinity elected Newton a minor fellow, securing for him the life for which he was designed. And when he received his master of arts in July 1668, he swore to "embrace the true religion of Christ with all my soul . . . and also that I will either set Theology as the object of my studies and will take holy orders when the time prescribed by these statutes arrives, or I will resign from the college."[2] As it turned out, he would neither take orders nor resign.

To celebrate his new position, Newton visited London for the first time. What he did there, we don't know, but he was there a month. And although London was the home of the Royal Society, England's premiere (and only) association of natural philosophers, Newton paid them no visit. But at the time, the Royal Society could not have cared less. How could they? They didn't know Newton existed.

Newton and Wickins continued to modify their room. They installed furnaces for Newton's chemistry/alchemy experiments (the two disciplines were still one). These experiments occupied a significant portion of his time and money. Records show that, in addition to furnaces, Newton purchased substances such as "Aqua Fortis, sublimate, oyle . . . , fine Silver, Antinomy, vinegar Spirit of Wine, White lead, Allome Nitre, Salt of Tartar."[3] And while in London, he had picked up a copy of *Theatrum Chemicum*, an important six-volume collection of alchemical treatises.

Newton experts often point out that alchemy occupied far more of Newton's intellectual and physical energies than either mathematics or natural philosophy. But Newton saw alchemy as *part* of natural philosophy. For one thing, many of his chemical and alchemical studies focused on the fundamental nature of matter. For another thing, these studies influenced his views on gravity to the extent that, without his study of alchemy, there may have been no theory of gravity. And of course, his knowledge of elements and compounds aided him in designing experiments and making equipment. His familiarity with metals, for example, aided him in shaping and polishing the mirrors of his famous reflecting telescopes.

Apparently, the status of fellow made few requirements on Newton's time, and he was, by and large, left pleasantly alone. Trinity, however, did assign him as tutor to one St. Leger

Scroope. Because Scroope was a fellow commoner—a wealthy student who ate at the fellows' table—and paid a large tuition, this assignment was an envied one, and usually reserved for the more senior or influential fellows. Scroope never officially enrolled in the college and, of course, never graduated. We know little else about him. As far as we know, he and Newton had little beyond financial dealings. This was, no doubt, an agreeable arrangement for both student and teacher.

One of the few people who we know interacted with Newton during this period early in his professional career was Isaac Barrow, the Lucasian Professor whose inaugural lectures Newton had attended as an undergraduate. Barrow was the only person at the college—at the university, even—who could understand Newton's work in mathematics and natural philosophy. Tradition tells us that it was Barrow who taught Newton mathematics, but by all accounts this is unlikely, and there is certainly no direct evidence for it. Later in life, Newton dimly recalled that he *may* have been inspired by Barrow's Lucasian lectures toward ideas related to calculus. Other than that, Newton could not say.

Barrow supposedly had three faults. He preached too long, smoked too much, and took too little care of his appearance. In the case of the first flaw, his sermons could reach three and a half hours long. But their content was edifying, no doubt, with titles like "Of Quietness and doing our own Business,"[4] and "Of Evil-Speaking in general."[5] Perhaps the longer sermons touched on the many virtues of patience.

As Lucasian Professor, Barrow was required to lecture once a week during the three academic terms, and to submit copies of his lectures in the university library. Although he lectured, he did so for only a single term per year, as would Newton when he succeeded Barrow as Lucasian professor. This might seem like nothing more than irresponsibility, but in all fairness, students rarely attended lectures at Cambridge. The tutorial system had taken over, and professors often found themselves lecturing to empty halls. Earlier in Barrow's career, when he was Regius Professor of Greek, his lectures were similarly attended. Frank Manuel notes that on the anniversary of his inaugural lecture as Regius Professor of Greek, Barrow commented, "Since you bade me that long farewell a year ago I have sat on my Chair incessantly alone—I am sure none of you will, as an eye-witness, challenge the accuracy of that statement even if I should be lying."[6]

We have good assurance, then, that Barrow knew Newton when the latter was an undergraduate, for it is conceivable that there were times when only Newton and Barrow were present. In any case, Newton and Barrow were the only two at Cambridge who were familiar with developments in contemporary mathematics and natural philosophy. Barrow would be the one to introduce the academic world to Newton. Newton's feelings about this introduction would be ambivalent at best.

Sometime after Newton had become a fellow, Barrow asked him to edit his lectures on optics, lectures given in 1667 (*Lectiones XVIII*). Although Newton made two small changes, surprisingly, he said nothing of Barrow's orthodox theory of colors, which Newton had disproved during the plague years. Some commentators suggest that Newton was deceptively and maliciously keeping Barrow in the dark. Some even accuse Newton of snickering behind Barrow's back. It is, however, quite possible that

Newton failed to tell Barrow of his discoveries because he simply didn't wish to reveal his findings in this setting—Newton, as we'll see, was notoriously reticent about making his discoveries known. Or perhaps he *did* tell Barrow, and Barrow decided to not make such significant changes. After all, Newton's findings were extremely controversial, and perhaps Barrow felt it would be better for Newton to reveal them himself, at a time of his own choosing, and in a context where he could do them justice.

For the rest of Newton's life, he had to be prodded to work on mathematics. Now that he had invented the calculus, he treated it like any other tool. But it was on one of these occasions of coercion that Newton was revealed to a circle of scholars outside of Cambridge.

Books are peerless for the one-way *dissemination* of ideas from one person to another. Books aren't, however, useful for a back-and-forth *interchange* of ideas. They aren't good for discussion. To discuss scholarly ideas, we now have academic journals, but in the seventeenth century, the primary means of academic discussion was by letters. This was beginning to change with the Royal Society's journal, *Philosophical Transactions*, but it would be some time before the *Transactions* became the primary means for dialogue. (And in the beginning, the journal often published bizarre topics. Gale Christianson relays, "Early issues of the *Transactions* abound with accounts of two-headed calves, werewolves, animated horsehairs, hermaphrodites, gargantuan tumors, and the birth of animals of one species to parents of another. One physician published 'An account of a Foetus that continued 46 Years in the Mother's Body.'")[7]

Early in 1669, Barrow received a book on logarithms—

Nicholas Mercator's *Logarithmotechnia*—from John Collins, a London mathematician. Collins fostered discussion among the mathematical communities in England and Europe by being the central hub of mathematical correspondence. He would sometimes solicit comments on mathematical works and distribute these comments to others in the field. In Barrow's response to Collins, he wrote that a friend here in Cambridge "hath a very excellent genius to those things, brought me the other day some papers, wherein he hath sett downe methods of calculating the dimensions of magnitudes like that of Mr Mercator concerning the hyperbola, but very generall."[8] Within days, Barrow sent to Collins Newton's *On Analysis of Infinite Series* (or *De analysi*), a work that also included Newton's method of fluxions. But because of Newton's reluctance to draw attention to himself, Barrow left Newton's name off the piece. Collins was absolutely delighted with the work, but he was perplexed by its anonymity.

In the meantime, Barrow encouraged Newton to let his name be known. Barrow's persuasion eventually succeeded, and on August 20, 1669, Barrow wrote, "I am glad my friends paper giveth you so much sastisfaction. his name is Mr Newton; a fellow of our College & very young . . . but of an extraordinary genius & proficiency in these things."[9] This is the first time any scholar outside of Cambridge had seen Newton's name.

Barrow also gave Collins permission to pass *De analysi* on to the Royal Society, but not permission to publish it in the *Transactions*. Society members, however, circulated Newton's paper in manuscript form, and his reputation began to spread among the mathematical community. Still, Newton had misgivings about the whole thing. He wouldn't formally publish the paper until he was sixty-nine.

Shortly after this episode, Barrow resigned from his Lucasian professorship. Because his resignation followed closely on the heels of the *De analysi* incident, it is traditionally believed that Barrow stepped down because he saw in Newton someone who far surpassed him in mathematics. But another theory proposes that Barrow—who considered himself more a theologian than mathematician—felt called to other things. Indeed, he left Cambridge to become chaplain to the king, although he eventually returned to Cambridge as the master of Trinity College. There is probably something to both of these explanations. In any case, upon Barrow's recommendation, Newton became Lucasian Professor of Mathematics in October 1669, at the age of twenty-six. It was one of the most lucrative and honored positions at Cambridge—those with endowed chairs wore scarlet robes to distinguish them from other fellows—and Newton held it for more than thirty years.

Although Newton's mathematical studies had been largely responsible for his succeeding Barrow, his inaugural lectures were on optics rather than mathematics proper. The statutes stipulated only that the Lucasian Professor must lecture on "some part of Geometry, Astronomy, Geography, Optics, Statics, or some other Mathematical discipline."[10] These lectures (*Lectiones opticae*, which he gave until 1673, at which time he changed the topic to algebra) would become the substance of Book I of his monumental *Opticks*, published in 1704.

As with Barrow's lectures, Newton's were poorly attended. According to Humphrey Babington—although this was fifteen years later—Newton's lectures were roughly half an hour, and if no one attended, he would lecture for only fifteen minutes. At that later juncture "so few went to Him & fewer that understood him, that oftime he did in a manner, for want of Hearers, read to the Walls."[11] It is ironic that even Newton's *public* engagements were private, as if to highlight his almost monastic nature. In any event, there is little reference to Newton's teaching beyond Humphrey's recollections. After Newton began working on his masterpiece, the *Principia* (published in 1687), he simply stopped lecturing.

In 1670, Collins was urging Newton to publish. On one occasion, Newton consented hesitantly, but with the qualification that: "soe it bee without my name to it. For I see not what there is desirable in plublick esteeme, were I able to acquire & maintaine it. It would perhaps increase my acquaintance, the thing which I chiefly study to decline."[12] Despite Newton's clearly stated wishes to remain unknown, Collins continued to tempt Newton with fame and prestige: "your paines herein will be acceptable to some very eminent Grandees of the R Societie who must be made accquainted therewith."[13] Collins would not hear from Newton for months. With silence, Newton told Collins to get thee behind him.

During this period (1669–70), Newton, in addition to resisting Collins's temptations, was back to his optical researches, clarifying the work he had done in Woolsthorpe. He refined his *experimentum crucis*, the telltale experiment showing that white light is not pure but rather a mixture of colored light. He performed his experiments with unprecedented precision. Using only a compass and his unaided eyes, Newton would painstakingly hunt down the source of minute measurement discrepancies of less than a hundredth of an inch. Westfall comments that "[n]o one else in the seventeenth century would have paused for an error twice that size."[14] Newton had extremely sharp senses, which no doubt aided him in these experiments. At the age of nine he could see the spire of a church on the horizon six miles away. Although in midlife he became nearsighted, his eyes corrected themselves. William Stukeley reported that "Sir Isaac's eyes were very full, & protuberant, which rendered him near sighted, in youth, & manhood. & was the reason of his seeing so well in age; the eye being betterd, by growing somewhat flatter."[15] Similarly, Newton had keen ears. Simply from the sounds of cannons in the distances, he once determined that the Dutch fleet had bested the English.

His interest in optics rekindled, he worked feverishly on his theory of colors. He even disciplined his diet to optimize his mental faculties: "to quicken his faculties and fix hs attention, [he] confined himself to a small quantity of bread, during all the time, with a little sack and water, of which, without any regulation, except that he took as he found a craving or failure of spirits."[16] Not all of Newton's missed meals were due to absentmindedness.

Earlier in the century, Galileo had used the refracting telescope to good effect. Newton's experiments revealed, however, that no matter how well lenses of refracting telescopes were made, images would always be distorted due to light's very nature. In response to this—and to test aspects of his own theory—Newton worked on a *reflecting* telescope, perhaps during 1669. He could eliminate these distortions by using mirrors, instead of lenses. The idea of a reflecting telescope wasn't new, but there were practical problems in their construction. For one thing, the viewer blocked the incoming light when looking at the mirror. Newton solved these problems, and constructed a small six-inch-long reflecting telescope that avoided chromatic aberration and magnified objects up to forty times, as much as a refractor many feet long.

Newton's telescope was the work of a craftsman as well as that of a scientist. One of the obstacles Newton had to surmount was polishing metal to the smoothness of glass. He also had to experiment with metals, making his own alloys out of tin and copper in his furnace. Near the end of his life, his niece's husband, John Conduitt, asked Newton about the telescope: "I asked him where he had it made, he said he made it himself, & when I asked where he got his tools said he made them himself & laughing added if I had staid for other people to make my tools & things for me, I had never made anything of it."[17]

Ironically, Newton would use a refracting telescope for his own observations of comets and planets. He was far more interested in his reflecting telescope for theoretical purposes. In fact, when it came to science generally, Newton cared far more about the knowledge itself than for its application in technology. For him, knowledge of God was all-important, and scientific knowledge was simply part of knowing God—knowing God through his works.

Just as Newton had nearly exhausted his interest in mathematics at Woolsthorpe, he never again completely devoted himself to optics after 1670. He would continue experiments here and there; and, like his work in mathematics, he would continue to elucidate his theory of light and color in papers, eventually publishing it in his *Opticks*. But no more would he attempt to make major discoveries or innovations. He had done what he set out to do. And still at this point, no one knew. He was twenty-eight.

At Cambridge, word of Newton's telescope had spread. And Newton told Collins of the instrument when the two met in London in 1669. Letters from those who saw it at Cambridge began circulating, as did Collins's accounts of it. Eventually, the Royal Society heard of it and, in 1671, asked to see it. Late that year Barrow—to whom Newton had loaned the telescope— showed it to the Society. This masterful piece of work thrust Newton's name beyond the mathematical community and into England's wider scientific world.

The Royal Society of London for the Improvement of Natural Knowledge was founded in 1660 by a group of natural philosophers who had initially met to discuss the philosophy of Francis Bacon. The founders included the architect Christopher Wren and the chemist Robert Boyle. In line with Bacon's views, the Society's goal was to further "Physico-Mathematicall Experimentall Learning"[18] by creating a means for discussion and dissemination of such learning. It was the first step toward the modern institutionalizing of science, and the creation of a professional community that reached beyond the borders of cities, and even nations. The Society's work was "to be applied to further promoting by the authority of experiments the sciences of natural things and of useful arts, to the glory of God the Creator, and the advantage of the human race."[19]

The Society also adopted the Baconian-influenced motto *Nullius in verba* or "On the words of no one." This was primarily an indication that scientific knowledge was not to be built on speculative Aristotelian philosophy but, rather, by experiment. Frank Manuel points out that "[t]he *Nullis in verba* of the Royal Society applied only to the human, not the divine, Word."[20] The Society was dedicated to the knowledge of *God's* world, of *his* book of nature.

Henry Oldenburg—once the tutor of Robert Boyle's nephew—was the Society's secretary, the man through whom all the knowledge flowed in the form of letters. Immediately after Barrow had presented the Society with Newton's telescope, Oldenburg sent Newton a letter informing him of his candidacy to membership. Newton was elected to the Society in January 1672 and an account of the telescope published in the *Philosophical Transactions*. Newton wrote to Oldenburg thanking the Society ("I doe earnestly desire you to returne them my cordiall thanks"). But uncharacteristically he added that he had something to share, something that was better than the telescope, a discovery that Newton called "the oddest if not the most considerable detection which hath hitherto beene made in the operations of Nature."[21] This "most considerable detection" was Newton's theory of light, the very reason he made the telescope in the first place. Although Newton waited a month—he contracted a temporary case of cold feet—he sent his paper on theory of light to Oldenburg. He would soon regret it.

CONFLICT AND REGRET

The "paper" on light was actually a letter, written to Oldenburg. It was read to the Royal Society and published in the *Philosophical Transactions* as "A Letter of Mr. Isaac Newton, Professor of the Mathematicks in the University of Cambridge; containing his New Theory about *Light* and *Colors*" (or simply "Theory about Light and Colors"). Oldenburg reported back to Newton that the letter was "mett both with a singular attention and an uncommon applause."[1] It was Newton's optical work—and not his work on gravity and motion—that initially made his reputation. And it made it quickly.

Newton was twenty-nine, hair almost entirely gray. He had developed revolutionary ideas in mathematics, dynamics, and optics. Yet he was only now becoming known to the scientific community, a community he already outstripped. He had tried to keep to himself, but circumstances conspired against him and thrust him into the spotlight. Newton—the only child, the autodidact—wasn't at all comfortable with other people, or the spotlight they shone on him.

To make matters worse, the spotlight grew hot. Now that his work was visible, it immediately drew fire. Newton should have known this would happen, but he was surprised nonetheless. He had grown so accustomed to his radical ideas that, to him, they had become obvious.

Newton's "Theory About Light and Colors" contained two claims, both unorthodox in the seventeenth century. The first was that white light was not pure but a mixture of colored light. The second claim was that that light was composed of particles, rather than waves—Newton's corpuscular theory of light. For the former, he had very good experimental evidence—an *experimentum crucis* in fact; the second claim was merely a hypothesis, an *unproven explanation* of experimental phenomena. But Newton hadn't made this distinction clear. This uncharacteristic misstep would inaugurate a lifelong conflict with Robert Hooke.

Robert Hooke, the Royal Society's curator of experiments, was seven years older than Newton. The picture that history sketches of him is not kind. Throughout his life he was physically frail, even disfigured. One of Hooke's few friends described him as "of midling stature, something crooked, pale faced but little belowe, but his head is lardge; his eie full and popping, and not quck; a grey eie."[2] But, Hooke's friend continued, "He haz a delicate head of haire, browne, and of an excellent moiste curl."[3] At least Hooke had that going for him.

Like Newton, Hooke had lost his father early in life. In Hooke's case, however, shame and guilt accompanied his loss. Hooke's father—"a man of the cloth"—hanged himself when Robert was thirteen. Things only went downhill from there, Hooke's tormented spirit pathetically gnawing itself.

One contemporary recalled that "His Temper was Melancholy, Mistrustful and Jealous, which more increas'd upon him with his Years."[4] Manuel writes, "A diary covering the period 1689 to 1693, when he was over fifty and Newton was in the limelight, bears the stamp of a cantankerous, envious, vengeful man, given to outbursts of temper."[5] If that weren't enough, Hooke also took his niece as a mistress. If Newton knew of Hooke's weirdness, it certainly contributed to the rancor between them.

Hooke—again, like Newton—was fascinated with mechanical devices, a fascination that similarly translated into an experimental acumen. Hooke tirelessly performed mechanical and biological experiments at the Society's weekly meetings. At one meeting, he tested the effects of viper poison on dogs and cats; on another occasion, he asphyxiated a chicken in a vacuum (but a snake survived a similar experiment). Although apparently hardened to certain amounts of suffering in the name of knowledge, Hooke had his limits. After a particularly gruesome vivisection of a dog, Hooke vowed, "I shall hardly be induced to make any further trials of this kind, because of the torture of the creature."[6] In this, at least, Newton and Hooke could agree. Newton "paled at all forms of animal suffering."[7]

Hooke's knack for experimentation helped make his reputation as England's expert on optics. This is where the acrimony between him and Newton begins. The two main views of Newton's "Theory About Light and Colors" were in direct opposition to Hooke's. Within a week of Newton's paper on light being read to the Society, Hooke responded with condescending criticism. It wasn't that Hooke doubted the results of Newton's experiments—in fact, Hooke claimed that he had already performed them all ("as having by many hundreds of tryalls found them soe"[8]). Rather, the problem, according to Hooke, was that Newton's experiments didn't support his two hypotheses.

That word—*hypotheses*—irritated Newton. And Hooke wasn't the only one who had used it to describe Newton's views; Christian Huygens, the premiere scientist on the Continent, called Newton's two views on light "hypotheses," as did a Jesuit philosopher, Ignace Gaston Pardies.

To Newton's mind, however, using the word *hypothesis* revealed an egregious misunderstanding of his paper. He was offering not a mere hypothesis but an experimentally proven fact—at least for his view that white light is composed of colored light. Newton was very conscious of the distinction between a hypothesis—an unproven explanation among other possible explanations—and a proven fact. It was his understanding of this distinction that caused problems. He viewed the "scientific method" (as we call it now) differently than his contemporaries did. As in many things, Newton was already forging ahead in his view of how natural philosophy should proceed.

We are to use experiments, he said, to establish *facts*. The results of an experiment cannot be doubted. They are there for all to see, feel, touch, hear, and even taste (something we will see Newton dangerously doing in his chemical and alchemical experiments). Hypotheses, on the other hand, are used to *explain* experimental results. That is, hypotheses were used to answer the questions: *Why* do we get these results? Why does the world behave *this* way?

But in his paper, Newton had contributed to the confounding

of hypotheses and experimental results. Newton had yet to fully separate his view that white light is composed of colored light from his corpuscular theory of light. Because of this, he mistakenly believed that the *experimentum crucis* also proved the corpuscular theory. As he admitted later, his *experimentum crucis* could only be used to support the "impurity" of white light—it could not be used to support his particle view of light. He kicked himself for his carelessness. Never again would he repeat the mistake. But he would continue to pay for it.

Even when it came to the *experimentum crucis*, there was controversy—not everyone believed that it was a crucial experiment. Hooke, for one, claimed to have obtained the same results as Newton, but could account for them with his own theory. That is, Hooke claimed that Newton's so-called crucial experiment did not definitively prove his claim that white light is impure. But Hooke didn't *show* that there was another plausible interpretation of Newton's experimental results—he merely repeated his belief that white light is pure. To Newton, this was galling. He wanted Hooke to either explicitly say why the experiments didn't support the theory or produce experiments that provided contrary results.

This bickering continued, with Oldenburg as mediator, sending, receiving, and cataloguing the letters. Very soon, Newton regretted letting his theory see the light of day. The criticisms, he felt, were baseless, and in Hooke's case, insulting. Hooke was using his established reputation in place of a genuine argument. And in Newton's eyes, Hooke's theory was "not onely *insufficient*, but in some respects *unintelligible*."[9] It would be one thing to have sound criticisms leveled at him, but to be tangled up in useless debates that kept him from his other studies—that was simply too much. Newton's temper was beginning to flare. He had—just as he had when Arthur Storer provoked him in Grantham—tried to resist being embroiled. But he was losing an internal battle with his passions, allowing Hooke to draw him into one of the most famous conflicts in the history of science.

But for now, as he pushed back the anger, Newton struggled to extricate himself from the scientific community and its distractions. In fact, in 1673, he tried to resign from membership in the Royal Society. To Oldenburg, Newton wrote:

> Sr I desire that you will procure that I may be put out from being any longer fellow of the R. Society. For though I honour that body, yet since I see I shall neither profit them, nor (by reason of this distance) can partake of the advantage of their Assemblies, I desire to withdraw.[10]

Oldenburg, perhaps in desperation, offered to have the regular membership fees ignored. But the fees weren't the problem at all (neither was the distance between Cambridge and London), and instead of explaining his real reason, Newton simply let the issue drop.

But only a few months later, Newton tried again:

> I must, as formerly, signify to you, that I intend to be no further sollictous about matters of Philosophy. And therefore I hope you will not take it ill if you find me ever refusing doing any thing more in that kind, or rather that you will favour me in my determination by preventing so far as you

can conveniently any objections or other philosophicall letters
that may concern me.[11]

Newton was already engaged in correspondence that he felt
obliged to continue. But Oldenburg could at least refrain from
sending him any new letters.

Another incident in 1672 gives us a further look at Hooke's
personality. Gottfried Wilhelm Leibniz visited the Royal Society,
showing them his new calculating machine. True to what will
become form, Hooke claimed to have already invented something similar—but better. Hooke had the peculiar talent of
getting others to unwittingly announce his discoveries for him.

In 1673, Newton stopped lecturing on optics, beginning a
lecture series on algebra. Perhaps he changed topics in response
to his growing distaste for a subject matter over which he was
constantly fighting. In any event, he would lecture on algebra
until 1683, after which he gave up lecturing altogether. But
because the material in these lectures is so advanced, scholars
are astonished that any student could have understood it. Of
course, if Newton was lecturing to the walls, the material's dif-
ficulty would have hardly mattered.

Newton still tried desperately to recover his solitude and
the freedom of uninterrupted study. Whenever contact with
Newton was attempted, he either ignored it or impatiently—
almost frantically—responded that he was busy with other
things. Neither mathematics nor optics nor mechanics held
his interest. He had moved on to other things—alchemy and
theology. But he had revealed his work in mathematics and
optics, and the world would not let him hide his talents. He

tried to keep his head down, nonetheless. And sometimes it worked.

But not always. In 1674, another annoying series of letters was begun by an aging—and most likely senile—English Jesuit, Father Linus. In a letter to Oldenburg, Linus flatly challenged the results of Newton's experiments. (Linus had famously questioned Robert Boyle's experimental results a decade earlier.) Oldenburg was either unable or unwilling to leave Newton alone and sent him Linus's letter. After two months of sitting on the letter, Newton replied, "I am sorry you put your self to the trouble of transcribing Mr. Linus's conjecture, since (besides that it needs no answer) I have long since determined to concern my self no further about the promotion of Philosophy."[12]

In 1675, Newton visited London again. But while there, he made his first visit to the Royal Society, discovering that the members held him in very high esteem, despite what the flurry of critical letters might indicate. This reception, suggests Richard Westfall, convinced Newton to reengage the scientific community. Not only did Newton respond to Father Linus, he also told Oldenburg that he had something further to share with the Royal Society, something he had written in 1672, back when he wrote his "Theory of Light and Colors." It would, he said, clarify his views on light.

Oldenburg responded with delight, and Newton, in December 1675, sent Oldenburg two (modified) papers, a "Discourse of Observations" and "An Hypothesis Explaining the Properties of Light Discoursed of in my Severall Papers." In the latter paper, "Hypothesis," Newton made sure this time to use his hypotheses as explanations, rather than advertising them as experimentally proven facts. In particular, he used his corpuscular hypothesis merely to *explain why* white light was impure.

Newton also noted in the "Hypothesis" that it was Hooke's 1672 critique that instigated it in the first place. Throughout the paper, Newton made frequent mention of Hooke, using Hooke's views as a foil for Newton's own. After all, Newton had arrived at some of his own views in direct response to those he found in Hooke's *Micrographia*. But Newton provoked Hooke further—he pointed out that some of Hooke's "discoveries" had already been made by other scientists.

The "Hypothesis" became an immediate topic of discussion at the Society's meetings. Hooke, already mindful of what he saw as Newton's earlier encroachment on his optical territory—a territory now shrinking—stood and replied that most of the "Hypothesis" was already contained in Hooke's own *Micrographia*, "which Mr. Newton had only carried farther in some particulars."[13]

Hooke and Oldenburg had been at odds for some time regarding other matters, and this was a perfect opportunity for Oldenburg to make problems for Hooke as well as reengage Newton. Oldenburg immediately sent Newton a report of Hooke's response (the report has not survived). Hooke was well aware of this possibility and so wrote directly to Newton, bypassing Oldenburg's mediation. This was, Christianson points out, the first letter to Newton from a scientist that hadn't gone through Oldenburg. In the letter, Hooke began, "These to my much esteemed friend, Mr. Isaak Newton."[14] He went on to propose that he and Newton correspond privately, to avoid any further escalation of hostilities, hostilities that may have been the result of "sinister practices" of someone who would go unnamed.[15] (Hooke meant Oldenburg, and Newton knew it.) Hooke continued: "the collision of two hard-to-yield contenders may produce light, [yet] if they be put together by the ears of other's hands and incentives, it will [produce rath]er ill concomitant heat, which serves for no other use . . . but kindle—cole."[16]

In February 1676, Newton responded with similar courtesy (calling Hooke "honoured friend"), writing, "What Descartes did was a good step. You have added much several ways, and especially in considering the colours of thin plates. *If I have seen farther, it is by standing on the shoulders of giants.*"[17]

For whatever reason, the proposed correspondence between Hooke and Newton never took place, but Newton bought himself some temporary peace—peace from Hooke at least.

A few months earlier, in the latter half of 1675, the young German philosopher Gottfried Wilhelm Leibniz had just discovered the method of differential calculus, some ten years after Newton. Leibniz was probably the one man in Europe who could be called Newton's intellectual equal. He, too, had, in only a few years, gone from student to master in mathematics. One of Leibniz's strengths—a virtue that Newton valued little—was an obsession to make his theory clear and user-friendly. He spent years on this, employing others to help him clarify his method. As a result, we still use Leibniz's notation of the calculus.

Leibniz wrote to Oldenburg, asking for a demonstration of two mathematical series, a request that Oldenburg passed on to Newton. Very reluctantly, Newton replied to Leibniz. Although it was a brief correspondence, Newton's two letters—written in 1676—have become famous. The first one is the *Epistola prior*, the second, the *Epistola posterior*. Newton still held his cards close, answering Leibniz's inquiries without giving away the store. He wrote in code: "The foundation of these operations is evident enough, in fact; but because I cannot proceed with the explanation of it now, I have preferred to conceal it thus: 6accdæ-13eff7i3l9n4o4qrr4s8t12ux."[18] This was, in fact, the fundamental theorem of the calculus. Coding one's discoveries wasn't uncommon (Hooke, too, had done something similar) and was used as insurance in priority disputes.

But despite Newton's coyness, he revealed enough to impress Leibniz, who gushed that "Newton's discoveries are worthy of his genius."[19] In between receiving the first and second *epistola*, however, Leibniz visited London, where he met with John Collins, who had a copy of Newton's mathematical paper, *De analysi*. Collins was so taken with Leibniz's obvious genius that he showed Leibniz the paper. Today we believe that this contributed nothing to Leibniz's development of his calculus, but the incident would complicate the priority dispute between Leibniz and Newton later in the century. Realizing his mistake, Collins kept his mouth shut (as did Leibniz), and Newton found out about the incident only after the priority dispute turned ugly.

The correspondence with Leibniz shows Newton's impatience with mathematics: "For I write rather shortly because these theories long ago began to be distasteful to me, to such an extent that I have now refrained from them for nearly five years."[20] And to Oldenburg he wrote, "For having other things in my head, it proves an unwelcome interruption to me to be at this time put upon considering these things . . . I am in great hast, Yours . . ."[21]

Unfortunately, Newton's correspondence with Father Linus continued to drag on, and Newton's frustration is apparent in a November 1676 letter to Oldenburg: "I see I have made my self a slave to philosophy, but if I get free of Mr Linus's business, I will resolutely bid adieu to it eternally."[22] Try as he might, it was a resolution Newton could never keep.

Oldenburg died in 1677 (the same year Barrow died). The man who replaced Oldenburg as Royal Society secretary— the man who would now be the mediator for all of Newton's Society-related correspondence—was Robert Hooke. There is no record of Newton's response to Hooke's new role, but he could not have been pleased. In any event, Newton had previously mentioned to Oldenburg the possibility of publishing a definitive work on optics, one that would conclusively support his theory. This, Newton hoped, would finally put an end to the disputes. Now that Oldenburg was dead, however, he would have to go through Hooke.

But tragedy struck, as Newton recounted to Conduitt years later. According to Conduitt:

> When he was in the midst of his discoveries he left a candle on his table amongst his papers & went down to the Bowling green & meeting somebody that diverted him from returning as he intended the candle sett fire to his papers & he could never recover them.[23]

Newton "was not himself for a month after."[24] His last bit of interest in optics was extinguished before the fire could be, and Newton waited almost thirty more years to publish his revolutionary optical discoveries. This event seems to have solidified his resolve to retreat into his Cambridge chamber.

The debate with Father Linus would not leave Newton alone, even after Linus's death. A Jesuit colleague of Linus's—a Mr. Lucas—took up Linus's fight, pestering Newton with questions and comments. We can sense Newton's weariness in a 1678 response to the news that there was a letter from Lucas waiting for him in London: "Pray forbear to send me anything more of that nature."[25] And with this, Newton slipped into the shadows.

8

"TO CELEBRATE GOD"

I n 1724, Newton wrote, "Its now about fifty years since I began for the sake of a quiet life to decline corresponden-cies by Letters about Mathematical & Philosophical matters finding them tend to disputes and controversies."[1] But as much as conflict bothered Newton, something else vexed him also. Ever since Barrow had revealed Newton to the mathematical community in 1669—and to the larger scientific community in 1672—Newton had been forced to discuss and defend his theories. And these "correspondencies" had confiscated his life, distracting him from what he really wanted to do: theology and alchemy. Yet despite the distractions, Newton still spent far more time on these subjects than in any other area. It was just that he wanted to spend *more* time on them.

Newton's study of theology and alchemy comes as a shock to people. But Newton was a great synthesizer; he didn't merely want to master a few separate disciplines. A command of math-ematics and natural philosophy was only a part of his goal. Newton endeavored to a great, comprehensive system of the world—from the solar system to the fundamental nature of matter to God's work in redemptive history. Newton's agenda was far more ambitious than it had a right to be, but inordinate ambition is common among geniuses.

We would now say that Newton sought a "worldview." But we use "worldview" too lightly to identify it with Newton's goal. Newton aimed very high indeed, and at the end of his life, he realized he had come nowhere near his ideal. (And what mortal could fault him for falling short?) Not long before he died, he said:

> I do not know what I may appear to the world, but to myself
> I seem to have been only like a boy playing on the seashore,
> and diverting myself in now and then finding a smoother
> pebble or prettier shell than ordinary, whilst the great ocean
> of truth lay all undiscovered before me.[2]

Some of Newton's biographers believe that Newton is simply expressing false humility. After all, Newton knew full well the enormity of his accomplishments. But this interpretation seems wrong. Given Newton's true goal of piecing together a theory of *everything*, he is merely stating the facts. Most of the truth remained far outside his ken, and he knew it.

All men, Aristotle said, desire to know. But they aren't all motivated to know for the same reasons. The ultimate goal of Newton's studies was to know God and "give him honour & glory."[3] In fact, for Newton, natural philosophy's main benefit was not the improvement of man's earthly condition; that was the Baconian view. Newton believed that all knowledge—including knowledge of nature—was, in the end, knowledge of God. Knowing was worship.

Although Newton considered all his studies to be part of his worship, theology held pride of place, occupying far more of his time than anything else. His theological writings take up millions of words; none of his other writings come even close to matching that.

But theology and genuine piety can quickly come apart. Theological acumen is not a very reliable indicator of faith. Yet Newton's religion was not an arid intellectual theory but a genuine relationship with the God of Abraham, Isaac, and Jacob. In Frank Manuel's words, Newton's Christianity "was charged with emotion"[4] and he was constantly attacking belief in a mere "metaphysical" God, the God of the philosophers. Newton wrote:

> To celebrate God for his eternity, immensity, omnisciency, and omnipotence is indeed very pious and the duty of every creature to do it according to capacity, but . . . the wisest of beings required of us to be celebrated not so much for his essence as for his actions, the creating, preserving, and governing of all things according to his good will and pleasure. The wisdom, power, goodness, and justice which he always exerts in his actions are his glory which he stands so much upon, and is so jealous of . . . even to the least tittle.[5]

To be sure, God's "metaphysical" qualities, like omniscience and omnipotence, are worthy of all praise, but Newton believed that it is God's person and his actions that especially command our adoration.

Newton was raised on Scripture, which inculcated a life-long devotion to it. He placed its authority above all others and knew it better than most divines. Despite taking the Church of England's authority very seriously, if ever he felt that the church veered from Holy Writ, he always deferred to Scripture.

We aren't sure when Newton began studying extrabiblical works of theology. It was certainly before the appearance of his earliest theological manuscripts of the early 1670s. His records do indicate, however, that when Newton first arrived at Trinity in 1661, he purchased Theodore Beza's annotated Greek New Testament and John Calvin's *Institutes of the Christian Religion*.

But in the early 1670s, Newton began studying theology with a new intensity. It is likely that some external pressure was being applied. Recall that when Newton became a fellow of Trinity College, he vowed to enter the ministry within seven years. This meant that he had to take orders no later than 1675. So in preparation for the ministry, he turned most of his attention (which was considerable) to theology.

As he usually did when studying something in earnest (and what other way could Newton study?), he began a notebook, with headings of the major topics he intended to study: "The Attributes of God," "God the Father," "God the Son," "The Incarnation," "Christ's Satisfaction and Redemption." The notes under these headings come almost entirely from Scripture. Newton approached his study of Scripture in the same methodical way he approached anything else, leaving very few stones unturned. He even collected various manuscripts of books such as Revelation, noting variant readings of significant passages.

But he was mindful that great minds had already considered these issues, and so he also studied the early church fathers. It is difficult to believe how extensively he read in the fathers. Richard Westfall writes that Newton not only "seemed to know all the works of prolific theologians such as Augustine, Athanasius, and Origen" but also was familiar with Irenaeus, Tertullian, Cyprian, Eusebius, Eutychius, Sulpitius Severus, Clement, Basil, John Chrysostom, Alexander of Alexandria, Epiphanius, Hilary, Theodoret, Gregory of Nyssa, Cyril of Alexandria, Leo I, Victorinus Afer, Rufinus, Manentius, Prudentius, and others. "There was," Westfall says, "no single one of importance whose works he did not devour."[6]

At some point in his preparation for ordination, Newton began to struggle with the doctrine of the Trinity. The Trinity was a topic of deep and heated discussion during the seventeenth century, and in the Anglican Church there was considerable division over it. (Deviations from Trinitarian doctrine within the English church were rampant.) Denying the Trinity was heretical, and so Newton remained extremely cautious about his views. Over his lifetime, he seems to have changed his exact position on the doctrine of the Trinity, but it is difficult to tell. Newton never discussed publically his beliefs on the Trinity, and his notes on it were not found until after his death.

We know, however, that Newton believed in the divinity of Christ and the Holy Spirit; he also believed that Jesus was the Messiah and atoned for our sins with his death on the cross. Newton even believed, contrary to Arianism (of which he is usually accused), in the eternality of the Son. He also embraced the straightforwardly biblical position that the Father and Son are one. What Newton did not believe, however, was that the Father and Son were one in the sense that they were *consubstantial* or of the same substance. According to Newton, the Father and Son were one, but this unity was not a metaphysical unity; rather, it was one of dominion and purpose.

There were a number of reasons for Newton's denial of consubstantiation. The most important reason for Newton was that he simply didn't see it in Scripture. Newton felt that consubstantiality was a metaphysical concept imported from Greek philosophy, a practice of which he was extremely suspicious. Consubstantiality was, he felt, a very shaky inference from Scripture: "All the old Heresies lay in deductions," he said, "the true faith was in the text."[7] Newton blamed both Athanasius *and* Arius for distorting Scripture when, in the fourth century, they "introduced metaphysical subtleties into their disputes and corrupted the plain language of Scripture."[8] Their ancient debate seemed to have more in common with Plato and Aristotle than with Jesus. Newton asked whether "Christ sent his apostles to preach metaphysics to the unlearned people, and to their wives and children?"[9]

Furthermore, the two main scriptural proof texts for the Trinity, Newton said, were corrupted by segments of the church to support the doctrine. In his letter to John Locke—"Two Notable Corruptions of Scripture"—Newton outlines how 1 John 5:7 and 1 Timothy 3:16 may have been altered. So, the shaky inference from Scripture to the doctrine of the Trinity was based on a shaky foundation.

Ironically, it was Newton's unswerving allegiance to the (genuine) words of Scripture that compelled him to deny consubstantiality and embrace what he saw as the true doctrine of the Trinity.

In addition to believing that consubstantiality was not a scriptural doctrine, Newton believed that the metaphysics underlying it "is unintelligible. 'Twas not understood in the Council of [Nicea] . . . nor ever since."[10] Just what is a substance, and what does it mean to be of the same substance (and not merely the same *kind* of substance)? "Substance" is a philosophical term that is mysterious at best. Like Locke, Newton believed that, even if things possessed some underlying substance, we know little, if anything, about it. And if this is so for ordinary material objects, how much more in the case of God?

As Frank Manuel writes, however, we must be careful to not "pigeonhole [Newton] in one of the recognized categories of heresy—Arian, Socinian, Unitarian, or Deist."[11] It may be that Newton himself never came to a final, clear position. This isn't surprising. The doctrine of the Trinity is *officially* a mystery, an article of faith that is incomprehensible. And the line between incomprehensibility and incoherence is often difficult for mortals to identify.

Newton's scientific methods spilled over into his study of theology. Notice that the doctrine of consubstantiality is an *explanation* of the biblical data, not a parroting of it. That is, the doctrine is a *hypothesis*, in the Newtonian sense. Newton, therefore, was not denying the original data—the words of Scripture—but rather the hypothesis used to make sense of them. Hypotheses are always less certain than the facts they are employed to explain.

But one thing *is* clear. Newton denied consubstantiality,

and this was enough to give him pause when it came time for ordination. How could he—while doubting what the Anglican church saw as a fundamental tenet (at least officially)—take a vow to support *everything* Anglicanism held dear? He therefore chose to resign as senior fellow of the College of the Holy and Undivided Trinity, and so from his Lucasian professorship. This was a brave thing to do: retiring from Cambridge would mean a lifetime of watching sheep wander his Woolsthorpe estate.

Newton attempted, however, to remain a member of the Royal Society. He wrote to Oldenburg, taking him up on his earlier offer to excuse Newton from his membership dues. After all, Newton's income would significantly decrease once he resigned his professorship.

But Newton made a last-ditch effort to keep both his vow to the college and his Lucasian professorship. This was the occasion of his trip to London in 1675—the trip on which he first attended a meeting of the Royal Society. In London, Newton asked the king himself for a special dispensation in which he could retain a professorship without taking holy orders. Newton knew that it was highly unlikely the king would grant his request—others had unsuccessfully made the same attempt—but he felt it was worth a shot.

The effort paid off. The king was willing "to give all just encouragement to learned men who are & shall be elected the said Professorship."[12] Newton was granted his dispensation and had again narrowly escaped the plow.

It was probably Isaac Barrow who helped Newton in this matter with the king. Barrow had been the royal chaplain in London and, in 1673, had been appointed master of Trinity

College. It is ironic, however, that Barrow would have helped Newton gain such a dispensation. Barrow had sworn to chase all forms of heresy from Trinity, especially antitrinitarianism. It is unlikely that Barrow knew nothing of Newton's views on the Trinity; as Newton's close friend and advocate, Barrow must surely have known why Newton wished to avoid ordination. The explanation may be that, on the one hand, Barrow realized Newton was still unsettled on the doctrine of the Trinity, but, on the other hand, agreed that questioning the doctrine was enough reason to refrain from taking a wholehearted vow to uphold it.

Although Newton withheld his theological works from the public, two were published posthumously: *Chronology of Ancient Kingdoms Amended* (published in 1728) and *Observations upon the Prophecies of Daniel, and the Apocalypse of St. John* (1733). Both works reveal Newton's fascination with prophecy and its fulfillment in church history. Prophecy, with its symbolic language, was much more difficult to interpret than biblical narratives, and so Newton developed a method to impose some semblance of rigor to the process. He borrowed one of the guiding principles from his study of nature. "Truth," he said, "is ever to be found in simplicity . . . it is the perfection of God's works that they are all done with the greatest simplicity. He is the God of order & not of confusion."[13]

Newton spent years decoding the symbolic language of prophecies, identifying prophetic events with those found in the biblical narratives and extrabiblical histories. He generated immense, detailed chronologies of world history and their prophetic counterparts. He attempted to describe the true, monotheistic religion of Noah, and its gradual corruption, which led to the pagan idolatries of Egypt, Babylonia, and Greece.

Newton also argued that, as Noah's descendents fell further from the true monotheistic religion of Noah, they slowly lost or corrupted the vast store of knowledge they had accumulated. We can see, Newton claimed, hints of this knowledge in the priest-scientists of ancient Egypt (surely aliens didn't build the pyramids), who hid their knowledge from the ignorant masses. Ancient Greek philosophers also had a store of secret wisdom. Newton felt sure that they knew about, for example, the calculus and the inverse square law of gravity.

But most of this knowledge was lost, and Newton felt a burden to recover what he could.

9

WISDOM OF THE
ANCIENTS

The idea of an ancient store of lost knowledge wasn't unique to Newton. This notion was popular during the Renaissance and still prevalent in the seventeenth century, and its adherents—usually alchemists—referred to it as the *prisca sapientia* or "ancient wisdom." According to this tradition, of which Newton was certainly a part, primeval priests-scientists were privy to nature's deepest secrets. This secret knowledge was passed down from adept to adept, in highly symbolic language—in code. As cultures spread over the globe, so did the *prisca sapientia*, although it was still limited to a select few. Egyptian priests, Mesopotamian magi, and Greek philosophers were all part of this tradition. And many alchemists traced their arcane knowledge to this tradition of lost wisdom.

Usually the transmission of ancient wisdom was traced back to Hermes Trimegistus or "Hermes the Thrice-Great." Hermes Trimegistus was the Greek counterpart to the Egyptian god Thoth, whom Egyptians believed had invented writing in the form of hieroglyphs. Some of the alchemists in Newton's time—Michael Maier, for example—believed that Hermes Trimegistus was an Egyptian philosopher-king and contemporary of Abraham. It was even possible, some alchemists said, that Hermes knew about the Holy Trinity. Newton would have certainly demurred on this point, as well as on other of the more exuberant "Hermetic" theories.

It's not clear what Newton believed about the origin and transmission of the ancient wisdom. He was well versed in the Hermetic texts, but he valued them primarily for their antiquity, not for their alleged source in Hermes Trimegistus. No doubt, Newton believed that Noah—as the sole link to the vast knowledge of the earth's pre-flood inhabitants—possessed all manner of practical and theoretical understanding. And we know that Newton believed Moses had extensive knowledge of nature—perhaps knowledge taught to him in Pharaoh's court by the priest-scientists. But more important, Newton said, Moses received scientific knowledge directly from God. For example, Moses knew a great many truths about creation but concealed its exact nature from the unlearned Israelites, intentionally leaving his Genesis account vague. But, Newton assured, Moses had done this without falsifying the account.

Without Newton's interest in alchemy, he would likely never have arrived at his theory of universal gravitation. His alchemy was part of his larger agenda in natural philosophy—to uncover important truths about creation and place them into a coherent system of the world. As Newton scholar Betty Jo Teeter Dobbs says, "His goal was Truth, and for that he utilized every possible resource."[1] And this goal was entirely in accord with the Royal Society's objectives, set out by none other than Robert Hooke in 1663:

> The business and design of the Royal Society is . . . To attempt the recovery of such allowable arts and inventions as are lost. To examine all systems, theories, principles, hypotheses, elements, histories, and experiments of things naturall, mathematicall, and mechanicall, invented, recorded, or practised, by any considerable author ancient or modern . . . All to advance the glory of God, the honour of the King, the Royall founder of the Society, the benefit of his Kingdom, and the generall good of mankind.[2]

We can even detect a reference to recovering the *prisca sapientia*. It was truth that these scientists were after, and if they could find it in ancient texts, then well and good.

But alchemy? It's difficult for us, as moderns, to reconcile our mythological picture of Newton as a rationalistic scientist with that of the mysterious and somewhat creepy alchemist. The alchemist of legend is an oily and greedy charlatan who claimed to transmute lead to gold; or perhaps your picture is of wizard-types with long flowing robes, faces shadowed by hoods, mixing unspeakable mixtures in a bubbling cauldron. To be sure, there *was* a lunatic fringe element in alchemical circles, as there were in the medical and astronomical communities. But these pictures of alchemy are the result of looking at alchemy through the lens of what we *now* believe to be true. Beginning at the Enlightenment, alchemists grew respectable, becoming chemists—we have demythologized alchemy into a respectable discipline. But much remains surprisingly the same between today's chemistry and yesterday's alchemy.

In any case, Newton and other like-minded alchemists were well aware of the eccentrics and sought to purge alchemy of its association with the fringe. Newton wrote:

> For Alchemy tradeth not with metalls as ignorant vulgars think . . . This philosophy is not of that kind which tendeth to vanity & deceipt but rather to profit & to edification inducing first the knowledg of God & secondly the way to find out true medicines in the creatures . . . so that the scope is to glorify God in his wonderful works, to teach a man how to live well, & to be charitably affected helping our neighbors . . . This philosophy both speculative & active is not only to be found in the volume of nature but also in the sacred scriptures, as in Genesis, Job, Psalms, Isaiah & otheres. In the knowledge of this philosophy God made Solomon the greatest philosopher in the world.[3]

Frank Manuel describes Newton's attitude toward the alchemical texts:

> Newton tried to de-mystify alchemical ideas, which were difficult to comprehend because they were enshrouded in mythic and symbolic language. In immersing himself in lengthy treatises on philosophical alchemy, he was looking for keys to the world of nature, preserved in cryptic religio-scientific formulas and allegories. But he did not find ultimate truth there; and

though he appreciated the moral purpose of the alchemists, whose writings are full of pious dedications of their work to the service of God, only the hieroglyphs of the Biblical prophecies themselves contained God's direct word.[4]

Again, Scripture was Newton's ultimate authority, and it directed his use of other sources of truth. We can also begin to see a developing theme woven through Newton's pursuits: truth hidden in symbols.

We must keep in mind that, in the seventeenth century, alchemy and chemistry were still a single discipline, sometimes called "chymistry." The "chemists" of those times were *alchemists* ("al" is Arabic for "the"). For example, Robert Boyle, one of the fathers of modern chemistry and the discoverer of many important properties of gases (e.g., Boyle's law), was at first Newton's primary source of alchemical ideas. Boyle and Newton maintained a lifelong correspondence that centered on chymistry.

There was, then, only *legitimate* alchemy and *illegitimate* alchemy. And even what was classified as "legitimate" in the seventeenth century can cause us to scratch our heads today. Nevertheless, contemporary physics has finally discovered a way to transmute metals. Unfortunately, using particle accelerators to turn lead into gold is cost prohibitive.

Alchemists believed that all substances were composed of a single, universal substance. The differences between metals, say, arose from the different configuration of this fundamental substance or *prima materia* (prime matter). Thus, they concluded naturally, one metal might be transformed into any other. But they needed the Philosopher's Stone to do this. The Philosopher's Stone—not literally a stone but a fundamental *substance*—was what transmuted one substance to another. The Stone could also, it was believed, cure illnesses and extend one's life. Some alchemists thought it could purify people's moral character and heighten their mental faculties. The Philosopher's Stone was red, the color of blood, or life.

The worry, however, was that the Philosopher's Stone—and other ancient secrets—would fall into the wrong hands. Therefore, alchemists were a secretive bunch. They met together in private rooms and used pseudonyms when they wrote. Newton's pseudonym was an anagram of his Latinized name, "Isaacus Neuutonus." Rearranging the letters, he got "Ioava Sanctus Unus" or "Jehovah the Holy One." A few scholars believe that Newton was actually calling himself God; others see, much more plausibly, that his pseudonym was merely a motto of sorts: "Jehovah is the Holy One." The former view is simply implausible. For Newton, idolatry is the fundamental sin and so it is doubtful that he would equate *himself* with God. (It would be particularly difficult to attribute such brazen idolatry to someone whose conscience was so tender that he confessed to "reading the history of the Christian champions on Sunday" as a violation of the Sabbath.[5])

Newton was first introduced to alchemy at Joseph Clark's apothecary shop in Grantham, where he learned how to use a crucible and fire to mix medicines and balms. He kept this skill his entire life, treating his ailments (imagined or real) with his own concoctions. One such mixture was called Lucatello's Balsalm, a delightful mixture of turpentine, rosewater, beeswax, olive oil, and St. John's wort, flavored with red sandalwood. Another recipe found copied in Newton's early alchemical notebook was to be "taken early every morning so much in good wine as will give it a tincture till the nailes hair & teeth fall of & lastly the skin be dryed & exchanged for a new one."[6]

Newton's alchemical studies, however, didn't begin in earnest until the 1660s. It may very well be that he was encouraged to take this path by Barrow and the famous Cambridge Platonist, Henry More. During the 1640s and '50s, Barrow was part of an alchemical group at Cambridge, and More—who had years earlier attended Newton's alma mater in Grantham—was the tutor of the apothecary Clark. More had tried to convince Descartes to tone down his mechanical philosophy and was a vocal critic of the new science. The connection between alchemy and Newton's wariness of Cartesian mechanical philosophy is not coincidental, as we'll see.

During the *anni mirabilis*—the wonder years—Newton absorbed Boyle's alchemical work, *Origine of Formes and Qualities*. He later did the same with Boyle's *New Experiments and Observations touching Cold*, taking pages of notes. Although Newton met occasionally with Boyle in London, Boyle influenced Newton mainly through books and correspondence. Even prior to their first meeting, Boyle sent one of his books to Newton through Oldenburg, who wrote, "I herewith send you Mr. Boyle's new Book of Effluviums, which he desired me to present to you in his name, with his very affectionat service, and assure of the esteem he hath of your vertue and knowledge."[7]

In 1676, Newton read one of Boyle's letters in the Royal Society's *Philosophical Transactions*. Boyle claimed to have discovered a special "mercury" that becomes hot when mixed with gold. Boyle then asked for advice: should he make this substance known to the public? This is an odd question to ask in a journal intended to encourage the spread of natural knowledge. But there was a good reason for Boyle's reluctance. First, any attempt at transmuting metals into gold was punishable by death. If gold could be readily *made*, there would be severe financial consequences for England. Second, there was also the danger of tainting the purity of alchemy. Rather than remaining a proper means of glorifying God by attaining knowledge of the fundamental properties of matter, the art would be spoiled by the presence of base and avaricious pretenders. Newton responded to Boyle's query with the advice that Boyle should keep his discovery secret. Newton wrote that the new substance (the Philosopher's Stone?)

> may possibly be an inlet to something more noble, not to be communicated without immense dammage to the world if there by any verity in the Hermetic writers, therefore I question not but that the great wisdom of the noble Author will sway him to high silence till he shall be resolved of what consequence the thing may be.[8]

Alchemists were afraid of opening a Pandora's box upon the world. And Newton, in particular, was secretive by nature, always concerned about the results of revealing his own discoveries. No wonder he counseled Boyle to keep his discovery quiet.

Although alchemical texts were important to Newton, they were merely guides. Just as in his optical work, the substantive discoveries were made by experimentation. Newton conducted alchemical experiments for most of his adult life. And like all his experimentation, his dexterity and proficiency were aston-ishing. He knew a remarkable amount about furnaces, even building and installing his own in his Trinity chambers. He and Wickins would keep the fires going continually. His later room-mate and secretary Humphrey Newton reported that Newton

> very rarely went to Bed, till 2 or 3 of the clock, sometimes not till 5 or 6, lying about 4 or 5 hours, especailly at spring & ffall of the Leaf, at which Times he us'd to imploy about 6 weeks in his Elaboratory, the ffire scarcely going out either Night or Day, he siting up one Night, as I did another till he had finished his Chymical Experiments, in the Performances of which he was the most accurate, strict, exact: What his Aim might be, I was not able to penetrate into but his Paine, his Diligence at those sett times, made me think, he aim'd at somthing beyond the Reach of humane Art & Industry.[9]

The "Paine" and "Diligence" referred to are seen in the accu-racy of his measurements. Newton would measure powdered substances not only by the grain but by the fraction of the grain, cutting them "with the point of a knife."[10]

But, unbeknownst to Newton, there were dangers. He con-stantly handled mercury, slowly poisoning himself. One time, when Wickins commented to Newton about his prematurely gray hair, saying that it was from thinking so deeply, Newton jokingly replied that it was from his many experiments with mercury. Recently, a lock of hair supposedly belonging to Newton tested positively for mercury poisoning. Despite the dangers, however, Newton became the world expert in alchemy. He was now the leading authority in mathematics, optics, and alchemy. He would soon add mechanics to the list.

There is a direct connection between Newton's alchemy and his other scientific work. Early in his career, he was a full-blooded mechanical philosopher. Descartes' work had convinced him that all motion in the cosmos was caused by matter coming into direct contact with other matter. Eventually, however, Newton became suspicious of a world in which inert matter was entirely separate from any sort of active principle or spirit. Descartes had divided the world into two categories—matter and souls. Humans were composed of both. A human's body was composed entirely of inert matter. The soul, on the other hand, was an active substance, the pilot of the body or a "ghost in the machine." Animals, the Cartesians said, did not have souls and so were merely complicated machines. In the Cartesian cosmos, there were no hidden (what the natural philosophers would call "occult") principles, no vital spirit, only matter and souls.

Newton, however, believed that animals were endowed with active spirit—perhaps not a soul, but an active principle nonetheless. He even entertained the possibility that matter had been given something like spirit: "God who gave Animals self motion beyond our understanding is without doubt able to implant other principles of motion in bodies which we may understand as little."[11]

Along with Henry More, Newton believed that the Cartesian mechanical philosophy led to a view in which matter was entirely independent of God. If Cartesianism was taken seriously, they believed, it would naturally lead to atheism.

Furthermore, an inert physical universe went entirely against the alchemical outlook, in which nature is alive or at least endowed with active principles. Whereas the mechanical philosophers worked to rid the universe of hidden powers, Newton saw no way of explaining many physical phenomena without positing undetectable active principles. Active principles, he believed, were required to explain how material objects cohere and how planets remain in their orbits. For Newton—and for us—gravity is a mysterious force with no empirically discernible cause. Without alchemy and its active principles, Newton may have never completed his theory of gravity, being trapped forever in Cartesian vortices of ether. And although it took years for Newton to extricate himself from these vortices, he eventually escaped.

Let us return to an important theme running through Newton's studies—truth veiled in symbols. There is an uncanny similarity between Newton's theology, chemistry, mathematics, and physics. Underlying all of these was Newton's belief that their secrets were accessible but enciphered. Newton saw himself as a cryptographer, a code cracker. The language of prophecy was highly symbolic, and Newton spent a lifetime interpreting it, translating it systematically and methodically in order to understand God and his actions in history. Alchemical language was uncannily similar to that of prophecy, but used a different set of symbols. The language of nature is also symbolic, as philosophers from

Pythagoras to Plato to Galileo had known. In this case, however, the symbols themselves were still in the making, and Newton had to complete the language. His own calculus became the prophetic language of the natural philosophers.

It still is today. Now that scientists are investigating reality far removed from the reach of our senses, they have to rely almost entirely on mathematics to point the way in their research. Experiments can only confirm *observable* phenomena. Mathematics guides physicists in the unobservable realm. And surprisingly, mathematics has been a remarkably reliable guide. For all the world, the cosmos looks suspiciously user-friendly.

And Newton reveled in this user-friendliness. He depended on it. The world was full of mysteries, but mysteries put there to be solved. Newton was a detective in a world that was far more than it seemed; the reality of it all outstripped the phenomena. The world is magical, supernatural. In his famous essay "Newton, the Man," John Maynard Keynes summarized Newton in the following way:

> Because he looked on the whole universe and all that is in it as a riddle, as a secret which could be read by applying pure thought to certain evidence, certain mystic clues which God had laid about the world to allow a sort of philosopher's treasure hunt to the esoteric brotherhood. He believed that these clues were to be found partly in the evidence of the heavens and in the constitution of elements . . . but also partly in certain papers and traditions handed down by the brethren in an unbroken chain back to the original cryptic revelation in Babylonia. He regarded the universe as a cryptogram set by the Almighty—just as he

himself wrapt the discovery of the calculus in a cryptogram when he communicated with Leibniz. By pure thought, by concentration of mind, the riddle, he believed, would be revealed to the initiate.[12]

Most modern scientists pride themselves on having purged themselves of thoughts of mystery and magic, while unwittingly using theories that are as mystical as they are "scientific." Newton, believing that the world is full of magic, found that it *is* full of magic. He, in turn, revealed some of his discoveries to us. But probably not all of them. In later years, he burned boxes and boxes of his own writings. Perhaps he was afraid of them falling into the wrong hands.

PHILOSOPHY
CALLS AGAIN

We now see why Newton wanted to be left alone: he was trying to unravel a mystery, untangling the world's symbols and weaving them into a cloth. And although he had been irritated by incessant interruptions, in 1678 he was finally able to cloister himself. He was now pleasantly alone. And other than a few important exchanges with other natural philosophers, Newton remained incommunicado until the appearance of his great *Principia* in 1687.

In 1679, Newton's mother, Hannah, contracted a "malignant fever" from his half brother Benjamin Smith, whom she had been nursing back to health. Newton rushed home to care for Hannah and, according to Conduitt:

> sate up whole nights with her, gave her all her Physick himself, dressed all her blisters with his own hands & made use of that manual dexterity for which he was so remarkable to lessen the

pain which always attend the dressing the torturing remedy usually applied in that distemper with as much readiness as he ever had employed it in the most delightfull experiments.[1]

It's not clear what the torturing remedy was, but in any case, it was unsuccessful. Hannah followed her two husbands to the grave, and Newton buried her next to his father in the Colsterworth churchyard. Benjamin survived.

Newton remained in Woolsthorpe for almost six months, arranging his mother's affairs—affairs that were now his. One of the recalcitrant problems was a slow-paying tenant—most likely Edward Storer, Arthur Storer's brother. Edward's family was long overdue on their payments, and this wouldn't be the last time Newton had to petition for remuneration. Yet despite the difficulties with the Storers, Newton's estate provided him a significant yearly income. On November 27, 1679—with most of his affairs in order—Newton returned to Trinity a wealthy man.

Waiting for him at Cambridge was a letter from Robert Hooke. As before, when they last corresponded, Hooke was conciliatory, assuring Newton that "[d]ifference in opinion if such there be (especially in Philosophciall matters where Interest hath little concerne) me thinks should not be the occasion of Enmity."[2] As secretary of the Royal Society, Hooke was asking Newton to resume philosophical correspondence: "I hope therefore that you will please to continue your former favours to the Society by communicating what shall occur to you that is philosophicall."[3] And if Newton didn't presently have anything to comment on, Hooke was kind enough to provide a number of suggestions.

Hooke's main suggestion was his own theory of orbital

motion. Hooke believed that he could account for planetary orbits with a single force, namely, an inward "attractive" force. That is, there is no outward or centrifugal force keeping a planet from plunging into the sun; rather, the sun and planet are kept from colliding by the planet's tendency to travel in a straight line. We would call this tendency "inertia."

Newton's explanation was different from Hooke's. Although Newton, too, believed in a central attractive force, he also believed in an additional outward centrifugal force that exactly equals the inward "centripetal" force, as he would later call it. According to Newton's explanation, the outward and inward forces cancel each other, so the planet is in pleasant equilibrium. On Hooke's view, however—the correct view—the planet isn't in equilibrium, but is constantly being pulled away from a straight-line path tangential to the orbit. At every moment in its travel around the sun, the planet experiences a nagging tug, a plea for it to remain in orbit. By the time Newton began work on the *Principia* in 1684, he had adopted Hooke's view.

But in 1679 when Newton read Hooke's letter upon his return to Trinity, as if in a hurry to clear his plate of Hooke's "business," Newton replied the day after he returned from Woolsthorpe. As far as Hooke's hypothesis on orbital motion was concerned, Newton hadn't heard of it. But more to the point, he wasn't interested in natural philosophy. He wrote that, even prior to his mother's death, he

> had for some years past been endeavouring to bend my self from Philosophy to other studies in so much that I have long

grutched [begrudged] the time spent in that study unless it be perhaps at idle hours sometimes for a diversion . . . And having thus shook hands with Philosophy, & being also at present taken of with other business, I hope it will not be interpreted out of any unkindness to you or the R. Society that I am backward in engaging my self in these matters.[4]

And if that weren't clear enough, Newton concluded:

But yet my affection to Philosophy being worn out, so that I am almost as little concerned about it as one tradesman uses to be about another man's trade or a country man about learning, I must acknowledge my self avers from spending that time in writing about it which I think can spend otherwise more to my own content & the good of others.[5]

But in between hinting that he would like Hooke to leave him alone, Newton made the mistake of responding—in passing—to one of Hooke's questions about the rotation of the earth. To make matters worse, Newton's reply contained an error. And so Hooke took the opportunity to point it out in a second letter, extending the painful correspondence. Hooke was hopeful: he was finally drawing Newton back into Royal Society business. Newton was no doubt fearful of the same thing.

The correspondence touched on various topics but finally alighted upon one important question: given that the force of attraction between the sun and a planet (or the earth and the moon) varies with the square of the distance between them, what—*mathematically* speaking—would be the shape of the planet's orbit? Kepler had already shown—empirically—that the orbit's shape is an ellipse. But could it be shown mathematically?

Hooke admitted that he couldn't perform the calculations; after all, he wasn't a mathematician. But he was sure that Newton could calculate the orbit using his method of fluxions. And he was right. Newton actually carried out the inverse calculation: assuming an elliptical orbit, he calculated that the force required varied according to the inverse square of the distance. But he never bothered to send his results to Hooke—the only way Newton had been able to escape the cycle of letters was by silence. Hooke's letters, however, had piqued Newton's curiosity. But once Newton finished the calculation, his curiosity was satisfied. He wouldn't revisit the problem of orbital motion until 1684, when Edmund Halley paid him an unexpected visit at Cambridge.

There are two important issues related to the Hooke/ Newton correspondence of 1679–1680. One is the use of mathematics. Notice that mathematics was considered incontrovertible proof for the *physical* connection between elliptical orbits and the inverse square law. It is a curious thing that scrawls on paper— scrawls that represent thoughts in our head—would be taken as a definitive proof of any physical fact. After all, the mathematics doesn't say *why* physical things behave the way they do; it only *describes* the way they behave. Yet Newton and Hooke saw mathematics as an *experimentum crucis*. It was the definitive experiment without the experiment. This is the birth of the method of modern physics. And it went entirely unnoticed.

There was another important feature of the correspondence: Hooke and Newton couched their entire discussion in terms of an "attraction" between two objects. But attraction is a very non-mechanical notion, and therefore using it went entirely against the Cartesian orthodoxy. Newton and Hooke simply took for granted that the sun could act upon a planet merely by way of a force, without an ethereal intermediary. Hooke and Newton had, without even bothering to mention it, jettisoned the fundamental tenet of the mechanical philosophy, namely, that everything occurs by way of matter coming into direct contact with other matter.

Recall that the ether was hypothesized to explain planetary motion in terms of direct contact between matter. In Cartesian mechanical philosophy, all phenomena required a continual "chain" of matter extending from one object to another. The propagation of sound is a good example. We hear a distant bird because vibrating air molecules from the bird's throat strike adjacent air molecules, which in turn strike other air molecules, resulting in a chain of collisions that finally reaches the air molecules in our ears. In the case of gravity, the sun affects planets through a similar chain of *ether* collisions.

Hooke and Newton were using terms like "attraction" and "repulsion," rather than relying on ether and vortices. Such terms would eventually create intense opposition to Newton's theory of gravity. Action at a distance was the very thing Descartes wished to avoid. In fact, philosopher A. C. Grayling wrote that the Jesuits—by whom Descartes was educated—officially opposed noncontact causation: "Let no one defend such propositions as that natural agents act at a distance without a medium, contrary to the most common opinion of the philosophers and theologians . . . This is not just an admonition, but a teaching that we impose."[6]

Action at a distance had fallen upon hard times. It's surprising that Hooke would be comfortable with it. Newton's comfort, on the other hand, is understandable: he had borrowed the action at a distance from alchemy. According to Newton's theory of matter, material objects stayed together because their microscopic particles attracted each other across tiny gaps of empty space. And because—as Newton would later famously say in Query 31 of the *Optics*—"nature is exceedingly simple and conformable to herself," it is reasonable to assume that similar forces acted on a planetary scale.

Sometime during the late 1670s or early 1680s, Newton performed a pendulum experiment that, in Westfall's words, "demonstrated to his own satisfaction that the aether, the deus ex machina that made mechanical philosophies run, does not exist."[7] Yet another *experimentum crucis*.

In November 1680, low on the horizon and very early in the morning, a comet appeared briefly. Only a handful of people saw it, but many more heard of it. A month later, another comet appeared. No one missed this one. It was enormous, its tail as wide as the moon in the night sky. Newton studied it almost every night until it finally disappeared in March. Because Newton was nearsighted, he first used a single lens for his observations, later moving to a telescope as the comet retreated. In addition to his observations, he also began collecting other astronomers' data on the recent comets. He even contacted his old schoolmate Arthur Storer. Storer had since moved to Maryland in the colonies and was now an amateur astronomer. A few years earlier Storer had

asked Newton for help with some calculations; now he recipro-
cated by providing Newton with data from America.

In the seventeenth century, people still believed that comets
were foreigners, visitors to our solar system. As aliens, they failed
to follow our solar system's rules. Furthermore, it was thought
that comets traveled in straight lines, each comet passing through
our solar system only once. In February, however, Newton
received correspondence from the Astronomer Royal, John
Flamsteed, claiming that the "two" recent comets were really the
same. Like most people, Flamsteed had only heard about the first
one. But he had predicted that the "first" comet would return a
few weeks later, exactly when the larger comet appeared.

Unfortunately, Flamsteed's proposed mechanism underlying
his single-comet view was implausible. Like all natural philosophers of the time, he believed that the sun behaved like a magnet;
he therefore proposed that the sun first attracted the comet, and
then, by reversing polarity, repelled it once it got close. This
theory apparently interested Newton—he sent a long, detailed
reply to Flamsteed. But his response went entirely against con-
ventional wisdom: Newton argued that the sun couldn't be
a magnet because when magnets get "red hot they lose their
virtue."[8] Because Flamsteed's explanation was implausible to
Newton's mind, Newton dismissed the single-comet theory right
along with its explanation, and the conversation went no further.
While Newton's interest in a theory of comets continued, his
interest in Flamsteed did not, and Newton dropped the correspondence. Flamsteed would never forgive this slight.

Newton collected more data on comets. He also began to
entertain the possibility that the recent comets were the same. Of

course, Flamsteed's underlying mechanism was wrong, but there were other explanations for a single comet. Perhaps, Newton reasoned, the comet had gone *around* the sun, returning in the direction it had come. In 1682, another large comet appeared— the one we now call "Halley's Comet." Newton discovered that the comet didn't travel a straight path, as he would have expected. He applied to the comet the theory of planetary motion he learned from Hooke. Newton's results indicated that comets behave according to the same orbital dynamics as planets. They weren't, therefore, our solar system's illegal aliens; they were legitimate, law-abiding citizens. With this discovery, natural philosophy had worked its way back into Newton's life.

Although Newton's interest in mathematics had significantly flagged after the plague years, he was still Lucasian Professor and had duties to perform. For the last decade, beginning in 1673, Newton had lectured on algebra. But he had yet to deposit a copy of these lectures in the university library. It was probably because he had no copies to deposit. He had been without a secretary for some time. Wickins spent more and more time away from Cambridge and finally resigned his fellowship to marry and start a family. (Years later, Wickins and his son Nicholas would work with Newton to distribute Bibles to the poor.) In 1683, Newton arranged for a new amanuensis (and chamber mate) to replace Wickins: the misleadingly named Humphrey Newton. Wickins' young replacement was a graduate of Newton's alma mater in Grantham, yet he never matriculated at Cambridge or Trinity. He worked for Newton five years, partly during the time Newton was feverishly writing the *Principia*. Newton took the opportunity of having a new amanuensis to make copies of his lectures, and placed them in the library.

But Newton's interest in mathematics hadn't dwindled entirely. As with other subjects, mathematics could engage him if the right problem came along. The problem that grabbed him this time was more of an ideological one. As he was moving away from the Cartesian mechanical philosophy, he also rethought his estimation of Cartesian mathematics. Newton reread Descartes' *Geometrie* and began studying classical geometry. Regarding Newton's appreciation of ancient geometers, Henry Pemberton would say years later:

> Of their taste, and form of demonstration Sir Isaac always professed himself a great admirer: I have heard him even censure himself for not following them yet more closely than he did; and speak with regret of his mistake at the beginning of his mathematical studies, in applying himself to the works of Des Cartes and other algebraic writers, before he had considered the elements of Euclide with that attention, which so excellent a writer deserves.[9]

Now even more appreciative of Euclid, Newton chided Descartes for mixing algebra with geometry. Newton had become a geometric purist.

This is delightfully ironic. Descartes' analytic geometry—the combination of algebra and geometry—had made Newton's calculus possible. Calculus depends on the ability to describe geometric shapes with algebraic equations. Perhaps it was merely

Newton's growing animosity toward Descartes' natural philosophy—and what Newton saw as its inclination toward atheism—that tainted his view of Descartes' mathematics.

In any case, Newton had distanced himself from Descartes. The extent of their separation could not have been more evident than in the book that eventually ended the Cartesian hegemony. That book was Newton's *Principia Mathematica*, the greatest scientific work in history.

THE *PRINCIPIA*

At a Royal Society meeting in early 1684, Robert Hooke, Edmund Halley, and Christopher Wren discussed the most pressing question in natural philosophy. They did not know, however, that Newton had already answered it. In fact, it was the same question that Hooke proposed to Newton during their last exchange—namely, what would the shape of a satellite's orbit be if the attractive force varied with the inverse square of the distance? More specifically, what shape would one derive *mathematically*, given the inverse square law? Newton calculated the answer but never sent it to Hooke. As far as Hooke knew, Newton didn't or couldn't answer it. Hooke, on the other hand, claimed that *he* had made the calculation. He was waiting, however, for others to try it and fail, so that his work would be appreciated when he finally revealed it. Wren and Halley were rightly skeptical.

Seven months later, in August 1684, Halley traveled to Cambridge and presented the question to Newton. Newton casually answered: an inverse square law would result in an elliptical orbit. Halley was astounded. How did Newton know? Newton replied that he had calculated it and went to look for the paper. He couldn't find it at the time but promised to send the calculation along to Halley.

Halley returned to London and waited. And waited some more. Finally, in November Halley received Newton's calculation and much more. Newton sent a nine-page treatise, *On the Motion of Bodies in an Orbit* or *De motu*. Halley knew the nature of what he held in his hands and immediately traveled back to Cambridge to urge Newton to publish it. But Newton replied that it needed more work: "Now I am upon this subject I would gladly know the bottom of it before I publish my papers."[1]

In the meantime, *De motu* was in great demand. Flamsteed complained that he wouldn't get to see it until everyone else in London had. He had to wait a month.

Halley, too, would have to wait, but in his case, he waited on Newton's revisions of *De motu*. Orbital dynamics had seized Newton and would simply not let him go. *De motu*'s revisions would grow beyond anything Halley could imagine. They would eventually become the great *Principia*.

Humphrey Newton—who lived with Newton during this time—gave us a rare glimpse of Newton's quirks:[2]

> When he has sometimes taken a Turn or two, has made a sudden stand, turn'd himself about, run up the stairs, like another Archimedes, with an Eureka!, fall to write on his Desk standing, without giving himself the Leisure to draw a Chair to sit down in.
>
> He never slept in the Day Time, that I ever perceived.

I believe he grudg'd that short Time he spent in eating &
sleeping.

He very rarely went to Dine in the Hall unless upon
some Publick Dayes, & then if He has not been minded,
would go very carelessly, with shoes down at Heels, stockins
unty'd, surplice on, & his Head scarcely comb'd.

At some seldom Times when he design'd to dine in the
Hall, would turn to the left hand, & go out into the street,
where making a stop, when he found his Mistake, would hast-
ily turn back, & then sometimes instead of going into the
Hall, would return to his Chamber again.

These comments of Humphrey's paint Newton as a classic
absent-minded professor. Many scholars believe that he behaved
this way because he was possessed with what would become the
Principia. Without a doubt, Newton's complete absorption in his
work certainly contributed to his eccentricity, but Humphrey
lived with Newton a year prior to Halley's visit, while the
alchemical furnaces were still going day and night. It may very
well be that this is simply classic Newton.

Scholars also suppose that, during the writing of the
Principia, Newton ceased all other work. Yet this is speculation
based on the enormity of the *Principia*. We should be careful
when assessing Newton's limitations. Remember that, during the wonder years, Newton did far more than most mortals
could imagine.

His colleagues at Cambridge were well aware of the mind
that lived among them. While walking in the yard, Newton
would sometimes scratch out diagrams in the gravel walkways.

The diagrams would remain for weeks, the other fellows of the college walking around them, lest Newton's work be disturbed.

In April 1686, the Royal Society agreed heartily that Newton's growing work on dynamics should be published (at that time they had the first of the *Principia*'s three books). They charged Halley with the responsibility of carrying it through the press. The Society would not, however, be able to pay Halley for his troubles. Rather, they promised him leftover copies of the fantastically unsuccessful two-volume work *De Historium Piscium*, or *On the History of Fishes*. *De Historium* was the only other book that the Society had sanctioned. Halley was to publish Newton's work at his own expense.

Halley, however, was thrilled just to be a part of the *Principia*. He realized its significance and, in his foresight, could imagine the privilege of bringing it to light. The fish books were icing on the cake.

Halley wrote to Newton, telling him of the Society's decision, as well as an unfortunate development concerning Hooke. After Hooke heard the first part of the *Principia* read to the Society, he immediately cried plagiarism. Newton, Hooke said, had learned the inverse square law from him. Reluctantly, almost in passing, Halley broke the news to Newton: "Mr Hook has some pretensions upon the invention of the rule of the decrease of Gravity . . . He sais you had the notion from him [and] seems to expect you should make some mention of him, in the preface."[3]

That did it. Arthur Storer—who years earlier had experienced the explosion of Newton's pent-up wrath—surely would have warned Hooke. Unless, of course, he had known Hooke.

This wasn't the first time Hooke had angered Newton, but previously Newton kept his cool. This time was different. Newton immediately reviewed the correspondence of 1679–80. He wrote back to Halley, recounting how Hooke had previously published others' ideas under his own name, claiming to leave all but the tedious calculations undone. So then, Newton said:

> This carriage towards me is very strange & undeserved, so that I cannot forbeare in stating that point of justice to tell you further . . . he should rather have excused himself by reason of his inability. For tis plain by his words he knew not how to go about it. Now is this not very fine? Mathematicians that find out, settle & do all the business must content themselves with being nothing but dry calculators & drudges & another that does nothing but pretend & grasp at all things must carry away all the invention.[4]

After all these years of dodging the requests of others to publish his works, Newton finally decided to relinquish his greatest work to the world. No sooner did he do this than the very thing he wished to avoid befell him. He justifiably complained that "Philosophy is such an impertinently litigious Lady that a man had as good be engaged in Law suites as have to do with her. I found it so formerly & now I no sooner come near her again but she gives me warning."[5]

But Newton did more than complain. The *Principia* was to be three books, and he had submitted only the first to Halley. The second was finished, but the third was not. Newton declared to Halley that the world would not see the third. Furthermore, before he submitted the second book, he struck Hooke's name from it. Originally, Newton had acknowledged Hooke's contribution in the second book, calling him "the celebrated Hooke"—but not now.

Halley's heart sank. He needed to smooth things over—quickly. Halley wrote back, assuring Newton that no one actually believed Hooke's claim and that the Society was entirely on Newton's side. Furthermore, he praised Newton's work and told him what a calamity it would be if it were never made known.

Newton cooled down and apologized for his outburst. Yet he never gave Hooke the credit Hooke felt was due him, and the breach between them was never repaired. In fact, it has been deliciously suggested that, years later, when Hooke's portrait disappeared during the Royal Society's move, Newton was responsible. There is no evidence for this, beyond our love for a good story.

In any case, all three books made it through the press under Halley's tireless watch. On July 5, 1687, Newton received a letter from Halley, informing him, "I have at length brought your Book to an end, and hope it will please you."[6] Halley the midwife had finally delivered something spectacular.

The title of Newton's great work—*Philosophiæ Naturalis Principia Mathematica*, or *Mathematical Principles of Natural Philosophy*—signaled an attack. In 1644, Descartes had published his own *Principles of Philosophy*, and the similarities between this and Newton's title weren't lost on natural philosophers. Newton was making a direct assault on Descartes' mechanical philosophy (and on his analytic geometry as well). Rather than a speculative system of ether and vortices, Newton limited his results to those he could mathematically *prove*, which, it turned out, was quite a lot. At the beginning of Book 3, Newton wrote, "I have presented principles of philosophy that are not, however, philosophical but strictly mathematical."[7] No speculation or wild hypotheses.

In fact, Newton made calculations that explicitly showed vortices unworkable. But even without this, the *Principia* would have devastated mechanical philosophy. Newton's entire system was so beautiful, so coherent, so accurate that it simply overwhelmed Cartesian natural philosophy—exactly as Newton intended.

Newton took the attack beyond Cartesian science, to Cartesian mathematics. Without the calculus, the *Principia* would not have been. But without Descartes' analytic geometry, neither would the calculus. Surprisingly, however, Newton presented the *Principia*'s results almost entirely in geometry, *sans* calculus. Newton later said that he first arrived at the *Principia*'s results using calculus but then translated the results into classical geometry, which to him was the pinnacle of certainty. Newton even modeled the fundamental structure of the *Principia* after the axiomatic system of Euclid's ancient work on geometry, the *Elements*.

One might think that couching things in geometry rather than calculus would make the *Principia* easier to understand. Perhaps it did. But it didn't make it *easy* to understand. At the beginning of Book 3, Newton also explained that

> those who have not sufficiently grasped the principles set down here will certain not perceive the force of the conclusions, nor will they lay aside the preconceptions to which they

have become accustomed over many years; and therefore, to avoid lengthy disputations, I have translated the substance of the earlier version into propositions in a mathematical style, so that they may be read only by those who have first mastered the principles.[8]

Conduitt was later told by William Derham that Newton made the *Principia* difficult because he hated confrontation: "to avoid being baited by little smatterers in Mathematicks, he told me, he designedly made his Principia abstruse."[9] Hooke, no mathematician, was not even privy to many of the *Principia*'s arguments. Then again, neither were most philosophers and mathematicians, and the *Principia*'s reputation for inscrutability spread quickly. One Cambridge student, upon seeing Newton, said, "There goes the man that writt a book that neither he nor anybody else understands."[10]

Euclid began his *Elements* with ten axioms, or assumptions—geometrical statements that are not reasoned *to*, but *from*. These axioms are the foundation of his geometrical structure. Upon these ten assumptions, Euclid built a great edifice of four hundred propositions, or theorems. Newton, captivated by Euclid, also began with axioms—his famous three laws of motion. From these axioms—these assumptions—Newton built his entire "System of the World."

Newton's first assumption—his first "lex," as he called it, or law—is what we now call "the law of inertia": "Every body perseveres in its state of being at rest or of moving uniformly straight forward, except insofar as it is compelled to change its state by forces impressed."[11]

Unless a (net) force acts upon an object, it will either remain at rest or remain moving in a straight line at a constant speed. This wasn't new. Newton had learned it from Descartes and Galileo. Although at first he accepted the concept of inertia, he had abandoned it for twenty years. Yet he took it up again, which allowed him to accept Hooke's view of orbital motion (that is, a centripetal force combined with a tendency for a planet to continue in a straight line). There is no centrifugal force; it's a fiction. What inertia *is*, exactly, no one knew. And no one does. Presumably, it's real. It works, at least. Regardless, once inertia was in place, other things fell into place too.

Newton's second assumption is the famous "$F = ma$" law: "A change in motion is proportional to the motive force impressed and takes place along the straight line in which that force is impressed."[12] The stronger the force, the stronger the acceleration (and vice versa).

And finally, Newton's third law of motion—his third assumption—says, "To any action there is always an opposite and equal reaction."[13] When you push against a wall with your hand, the wall is pushing back on your hand with the same force.

From these three assumptions, Newton built. And he continued to build until he constructed the crowning achievement of his natural philosophy: his theory—his *law*—of gravity. This theory goes back to the *anni mirabili*, the plague exile in Woolsthorpe, twenty years earlier. The apple and the moon are "attracted"—to use that antimechanical notion—by the same force. This force varies with the square of the distance from the earth's center. This much Newton knew during the 1660s. And it was as revolutionary as it was secret.

But it took two more decades for Newton to mold the theory into something serviceable, yet bordering on inconceivable. Yet, while nearly inconceivable it was also beautiful and, furthermore, resulted in remarkably accurate predictions, from the appearance of comets to the unexpected bulge in the earth's midsection. It passed the empirical tests with flying colors. It matched the world. It saved the phenomena, as Plato would say. Or saved most of them, for no theory is perfect, and even the great ones have wrinkles to iron, messes that require mopping up.

Newton put his law of universal gravitation this way: "Gravity exists in all bodies universally and is proportional to the quantity of matter in each."[14] We now put it thus:

$$F_g = G \frac{m_1 m_2}{r^2}$$

More than any other, this is the "sole Principle" of the *Principia*.

One of the striking things about this equation is that it is not about anything physical at all. It is a symbolic sentence about numbers. To be sure, it is about the numbers we "attach" to physical objects, but it is marvelously mysterious just how or why we can do this. On the other hand, the law itself—if not the equation expressing it—is straightforward, but deceptively so. It hides something that no sane person would believe if the law weren't so successful at predicting how the cosmos will behave.

Since the wonder years at Woolsthorpe, Newton had come to believe other things about gravity, not the least of which is that it should be called "gravity," which used to mean a "heaviness" or "seriousness" of disposition. He also arrived at the conclusion that this attractive force was mutual, that just as the earth pulled on the moon and apple, both the apple and moon pulled back. And this was because, he further concluded, the apple and the moon were both sources of their own gravitational force. In fact, *all* objects in the universe have their own gravitational force. You and the book in front of you share a special connection—both of you exert a gravitational force on the other. Not only that, you both exert a gravitational force on everything else in the cosmos, and everything else reciprocates. Everything. Newton's theory of gravity is *universal*. It is a single law that governs rocks as well as planets, and it finally buried the Aristotelian view that there were two realms—one of the starry heavens and another of the earth. No longer were two separate theories needed; a single theory would do. The cosmos was now a *uni*verse.

Like many things we take for granted, gravity is ridiculous. We believe it anyway. But at first, not everyone did. In fact, the Cartesians—just about everyone on the European continent—erupted with ridicule. In addition to presenting his theory of gravity, Newton rejected the existence of ether and vortices, thereby rejecting the most plausible underlying *cause* of gravity. And—in the *Principia* at least—he didn't replace it with anything. And *nothing* was unacceptable.

DON'T ASK WHY

If there is no intervening material between the earth and the moon, how does the sun reach out and touch a planet millions of miles away? And how might a force affect a distant object *immediately*? If the sun were to instantly vanish, all the planets—at that same instant—would stop feeling the sun's attraction. But the sun's image, its light, would remain for a while. (From the earth, we wouldn't see the sun's disappearance for another eight minutes.) It takes time for light to travel. Gravity's effects are immediate. But nothing, contemporary physics tells us, can travel faster than light. Is gravitational force a *thing*, then? In the seventeenth century, the very notion of a force was mysterious. And although it is difficult to admit, we still don't know what a force is, if it is anything at all.

Let's drop the talk of forces and focus on the objects themselves. We see how an object can interact with another object through physical contact. When we pick up a ball, we move it by *touching* it. But when we release the ball, the earth continues to pull it down—without touching it. How can we account for this action at a distance? How can we *explain* it?

In the *Principia*, Newton didn't try. He was mindful of the distinction between a fact he could prove by experiment or calculation, and an explanation of the fact. The fact of gravity is plain. We feel gravity. Its explanation, however, is a different story. And in the *Principia*, Newton refrained from telling a story about gravity. As he put it:

> I have not been able to discover the cause of those properties
> of gravity from phaenomena, and I feign no hypotheses. For
> whatever is not deduc'd from phaenomena, is to be called an
> hypothesis; and hypotheses, whether metaphysical or physi-
> cal, whether of occult [hidden] qualities or mechanical, have
> no place in experimental philosophy.[1]

"It is enough," he concluded, "that gravity really exists and acts according to the laws that we have set forth."[2]

A century later, when the French mathematician and physicist Pierre-Simon Laplace presented a copy of his monumental *Celestial Mechanics* to Napoleon Bonaparte, the emperor responded, "Monsieur Laplace, they tell me you have written this large book on the system of the universe and have never even mentioned its Creator." Laplace coolly replied, "I have no need of this hypothesis."[3]

This story is often told in order to show that science has proven that God doesn't exist. But of course, science has not done this. The story does, however, provide something of an object lesson about the nature of science as Newton conceived of it.

Newton put *limitations* on science. He said that the methods of science should be limited to experiments and mathematics. But Newton was well aware that, by putting these practical limits on science, he limited what we could know through science. In the *Principia*'s preface he wrote:

> Since the ancients (according to Pappus) considered *mechanics* to be of the greatest importance in the investigation of nature and science and since the moderns—rejecting substantial forms and occult [hidden] qualities—have undertaken to reduce the phenomena of nature to mathematical laws, it has seemed best in this treatise to concentrate on *mathematics* as it relates to natural philosophy.[4]

Notice that Newton said he was limiting his scope to what he could show mathematically merely "*in this treatise.*" He did not for a moment think that the domain of science encompassed all there is, or all that is important. Natural philosophy—alchemy included—was only *part* of his worldview. Religion, theology, and prophesy formed much more of it, providing the ultimate explanations that science could not provide. Newton attributed the work of gravity, for example, to the direct action of God. But this didn't (directly) come from experiments or mathematics.

Part of Newton's reason for limiting the goal of science was to make its goal fit its methods. Mathematics doesn't explain *why* objects behave the way they do; it only describes the manner in which they behave. This isn't to belittle mathematics; accurately describing nature is no small task. It is astounding that this can be done at all, much less to the degree we do it. But consider the question, "Why are objects closer to the earth pulled harder than the same objects when farther away?" The answer is *not*: "Because gravity varies according to the inverse square law." This merely quantitatively describes what you already knew: all things being equal, objects are attracted less the farther away they are from the earth.

Newton wasn't the first to limit natural philosophy to description. Galileo had suggested this. Rather than attempt broad speculative hypotheses or explanations of *why* an object falls (for example, the Aristotelian explanation was that "earthy" objects had a built-in desire to reach the center of the cosmos), natural philosophy, Galileo said, should focus on *describing* how the cosmos behaves. Furthermore, he continued, our descriptions should be couched in the language of mathematics as much as possible, for God had written the world in such a language.

Newton carried this idea to fruition. He invented the mathematical language in which to couch the descriptions. In his "System of the World," Newton began with "phenomena"—things we can observe—whose behavior requires mathematical description. He then went on to describe the behavior with mathematics, quantifying it. In the *Principia*, Newton is therefore fulfilling Plato's ancient charge to mathematically "save the phenomena," to describe the appearances.

Plato believed that God orders the universe according to perfect mathematical laws, laws that are intelligible to human beings. Plato had learned this from the Pythagoreans. Through Plato, the Pythagorean view became natural philosophy's underlying assumption. And although Newton wholeheartedly accepted the view, it wasn't part of his *Principia*. Rather, his natural philosophy was underwritten by it. It was more fundamental than his natural philosophy—it explained it, made sense of it, made it possible.

Alexander Pope's epitaph for Newton, carved above the fireplace in the room where Newton was born, declares:

> Nature and nature's laws lay hid in night;
> God said, "Let Newton be," and all was light.

We can excuse Pope's extravagance. It was an epitaph, after all. But it is certainly true that, through Newton, God allowed humans to see things that had remained in the shadows for countless generations. The divine mathematical plan that the Greeks had only dimly seen was now evident.

But, remarkably, just as the *Principia* was a fulfillment of the ancient Greek dream, it was simultaneously the model for modern science. Natural philosophy quickly accepted the limitations Newton put on it. Laplace was right to tell Napoleon that he had "no need of this hypothesis." By Laplace's time, natural philosophy had already stopped asking *why* things behaved the way they did. From here it was only a short step to believing that the kinds of questions Newton put to natural philosophy were the most important questions.

This view spread quickly through Western culture and is now the dominant view. The twentieth century's most influential American philosopher, Willard Van Orman Quine, based his entire philosophy on what he called "naturalism," the view that science—particularly physics—provides the human race with all its genuine knowledge. If science cannot answer a question, Quine believed, then it isn't worth asking. Today, naturalism is rampant in philosophy and science.

The narrowed scope of science narrowed the scope of reality as well. It made the world smaller, and knowledge of the smaller universe became all the knowledge there is. With less to know, we know a much greater part, making it look as though we've taken a significant step toward omniscience, toward being like God. And this, of course, is what man has always wanted, beginning with the Fall.

This was not lost on Lord Byron. A century after Newton's death he wrote:

> When Newton saw an apple fall, he found
> In that slight startle from his contemplation—
> 'Tis said (for I'll not answer above ground
> For any sage's creed or calculation)—
> A mode of proving that the earth turn'd round
> In a most natural whirl, called "gravitation;"
> And this is the sole mortal who could grapple,
> Since Adam, with a fall or with an apple.
> Man fell with apples, and with apples rose,
> If this be true; for we must deem the mode
> In which Sir Isaac Newton could disclose,
> Through the then unpaved stars, the turnpike-road,
> A thing to counterbalance human woes;
> For, ever since, immortal man hath glow'd
> With all kinds of mechanics, and full soon
> Steam-engines will conduct him to the moon.

Newton became the new Messiah. Recently, the atheist Richard Dawkins suggested that since Newton was born on Christmas day, his birthday would be an appropriate alternative to celebrating Christ's birth. It would be interesting to see Newton's reaction.

IN FULL VIEW

The *Principia*'s public appearance was a watershed in Newton's life. Even before Halley published it, Newton was well-known. But he was now about to become the most famous intellect in the Western world. The *Principia* was a flare in the night sky, alerting Europe to Newton's genius. Newton's life would change forever. No more would his time be solely his own. He was forty-four.

While he was writing the *Principia*, Newton simply stopped lecturing, never to take it up again. Perhaps no one noticed. Furthermore, other professors had capitulated to empty lecture halls in the same way. His position as Lucasian Professor of Mathematics became a sinecure, a comfortable position that paid him for merely existing.

Newton continued to work on alchemy, theology, some mathematics, and a little bit of optics. He also continued to improve the *Principia*—nothing is perfect. But Newton would never again be caught up by the same creative stream that carried him along the first half of his life. The *Principia* would be his greatest work, destined to become one of humanity's treasures.

And it was immediately received with awe. According to Halley, the *Principia* is a divine work. In place of an editor's preface to the work, Halley wrote an *Ode on This Splendid Ornament of Our Time and Our Nation, the Mathematico-Physical Treatise by the Eminent Isaac Newton*. In it, he gushed:

> O you who rejoice in feeding on the nectar of the gods in heaven,
> Join me in singing the praises of NEWTON, who reveals all this,
> Who opens the treasure chest of hidden truth,
> NEWTON, dear to the Muses,
> The one in whose heart Phoebus Apollo dwells and whose mind
> he has filled with all his divine power;
> No closer to the gods can any mortal rise.[1]

Although embarrassingly effusive, Halley's praise accurately reflects how the *Principia* was received over the next century. Newton himself was seen as more than human. When Dr. John Arbuthnot showed the *Principia* to Marquis de l'Hôpital, the French mathematician, l'Hôpital

> cried out with admiration Good god what a fund of knowledge there in that book? he then asked the Dr every particular about Sr I. even to the colour of his hair said does he eat & drink & sleep. is he like other men? & was surprized when the Dr told him he conversed chearfully with his friends assumed nothing & put himself upon a level with all mankind.[2]

Most English natural philosophers were immediately convinced by the anti-Cartesian arguments in the *Principia*. Not so on the Continent. There was a healthy dose of nationalistic fervor on both sides of the Channel. The great Continental philosophers Huygens and Leibniz balked at Newton's rejection of ether and vortices. Leibniz wrote to Newton, "I noticed you are in favor of a vacuum and of atoms. I do not see the necessity which compels you to return to such extraordinary entities."[3] He also complained about Newton's refusal to "feign hypotheses" about gravity and its spooky action at a distance, writing to a friend, "He is admitting that no cause underlies that truth that a stone falls towards the Earth."[4] Leibniz believed that natural philosophy should include the very hypotheses Newton endeavored to avoid. (Of course, Newton was not admitting that gravity had no cause; he merely refrained from speculation "in this treatise.") Yet for all its anti-Cartesianism, Huygens and Leibniz were impressed. The *Principia* demanded their respect even where it failed to earn their allegiance.

Hooke, however, continued to claim that not everything in the *Principia* was Newton's. To the end of his bitter life, he seethed over the glory that he believed had been stolen.

As soon as Newton finished writing the *Principia*, however, he was caught up in a dispute that had nothing to do with natural philosophy. Two years earlier, in 1685, the Catholic king James II had ascended England's throne. Newton, along with most of England—and all of Cambridge—was bitterly opposed to "popery." The dispute arose in February 1687 when the king commanded that Cambridge University's Sidney Sussex College award an MA to Alban Francis, a Benedictine monk. Cambridge was a Protestant bastion, and so the king, as part of a strategy to spread Catholicism in England, tried to place an agent of change in the heart of the academy.

Newton's response was uncharacteristic of a cloistered academic. He immediately called for Cambridge to openly resist the king's command: "An honest Courage in these matters will secure all, having Law on our sides."[5] Most studies have shown that disobeying the king decreases human life expectancy. Newton, however, was willing to risk it all on this point.

Not surprisingly, the king was furious. He summoned a group of representatives from Cambridge. Newton was among them, as was Humphrey Babington. In May 1687, the representatives appeared before an Ecclesiastical Commission. But they stood their ground and only the group's leader—vice chancellor of Cambridge, John Peachell—was fired. The head of the Commission, Lord Jeffreys, told the rest:

> Gentlemen, your best course will be a ready obedience to his majesty's command for the future, and by giving a good example to others, to make amends for the ill example that has been given you. Therefore I shall say to you what the scripture says, and rather because most of you are divines; Go your way, and sin no more, lest a worse thing come unto you.[6]

The university's representatives returned to Cambridge with their jobs and heads secure. Two months later, Halley presented King James II with a copy of the *Principia*. There is no record of the king's response.

The king soon lost interest in Alban Francis. He was forced to flee England when Protestant William of Orange invaded with his troops in what would be called the Glorious Revolution. Newton, having taken a high-profile stand against James II, was now known for being loyal to the Protestant throne. His courage was rewarded, and in 1689, he was elected to represent Cambridge in Parliament. He began spending more time in London and sent Humphrey Newton home.

Parliament immediately proclaimed William and Mary king and queen over England. It also set forth a proclamation of religious tolerance to all but Catholics and anti-Trinitarians. Newton, it is interesting to note, remained silent during the session, except on one occasion when he asked to have one of the windows closed. When Newton served in Parliament again in 1701, he said even less.

In London, which had been steadily rebuilt after the Great Fire two decades earlier, Newton's social horizons expanded. (Newton would later be part of London's restoration, serving on a committee to build one hundred new churches.) There he met John Locke, with whom he became a lifelong friend. Locke and Newton would visit one another and carry on a lively correspondence until Locke's death in 1704. Much of their correspondence centered on theology (but also included alchemy). Locke remarked to his cousin that he "knew few who were Newton's equal in knowledge of the Bible,"[7] and he and Newton probably shared similar views on the Trinity. Recall that it was to Locke whom Newton wrote his anti-Trinitarian letter, "Two Notable Corruptions of Scripture."

Locke and Newton also agreed on the nature of philosophy. Locke saw the *Principia* as a practical outworking of philosophical views similar to his own. He eagerly read the *Principia* but was instantly stymied by the mathematics. Locke's friend Christian Huygens assured him that the mathematics was trustworthy and that he could skip the demonstrations. Locke prefaces his own epic work on epistemology, *An Essay Concerning Human Understanding*, with the remark that readers were then living "in an age that produces such masters as the great Huygens and the incomparable Mr. Newton."[8] Newton's influence on philosophers (not merely natural philosophers) cannot be underestimated. In fact, it is difficult to appreciate or understand the Enlightenment without a familiarity with Newton's work. The *Principia* set in motion the philosophy of Immanuel Kant, the Enlightenment's spokesman.

Newton's contacts in London continued to grow. He met Samuel Pepys, the president of the Royal Society, with whom he struck up a correspondence. Pepys once wrote Newton with a gambling question, asking him a mathematician's perspective on probability. Newton also met Huygens, the leading natural philosopher on the Continent. They discussed the controversial ideas of the *Principia*, and Huygens later said of Newton, "I don't care that he's not a Cartesian as long as he doesn't serve up conjectures such as attractions."[9] Newton once even dined with King William and entertained the idea of taking a government position in London. His influential friends began soliciting government appointments on his behalf. At first, they were entirely unsuccessful.

But Newton was becoming a man of the world, at least in contrast to his monastic lifestyle of Cambridge. He had his portrait painted by a leading artist, Sir Godfrey Kneller. It is the earliest picture we have of Newton. In his forty-sixth year, he has thin, chiseled features; long, gray hair; a cleft chin; a pointed nose; and large eyes. His fingers are also long and thin, evidence no doubt of the manual dexterity for which he was famous.

Robert Boyle died in 1691, and in his will he had endowed a lecture series "for proving the Christian Religion against notorious infidels."[10] The Reverend Richard Bentley gave the first series of Boyle Lectures in 1692, which he entitled *A Confutation of Atheism*. In preparation for these sermons, Bentley consulted closely with Newton, their famous correspondence providing insight into Newton's views on the relation between natural philosophy and religion. Newton was delighted to help.

Their letters focus on the divine design of the universe. In order to account for—in order to *explain*—the subject matter of the *Principia*, Newton required an intelligent supernatural being who purposefully created and continually sustains creation. For example, he told Bentley that "the motions which the Planets now have could not spring from any naturall cause alone but were imprest by an intelligent Agent."[11]

Outside of science, such hypotheses were encouraged and even necessary. They were, in fact, part of Newton's motivation in writing the *Principia*:

> When I wrote my treatise about our Systeme I had an eye upon such Principles as might work with considering men for the beleife of a Deity & nothing can rejoyce me more then to find it usefull for that purpose But if I have done the publick any service this way 'tis due to nothing but industry & a patient thought.[12]

Newton also mused about gravity. Although in the *Principia* he feigned no hypotheses regarding the cause of gravitational attraction at a distance, it was clear to him what hypothesis should be feigned:

> Tis unconceivable that inanimate brute matter should (without the mediation of something else which is not material) operate upon & affect other matter without mutual contact; as it must if gravitation in the sense of Epicurus be essential & inherent in it. And this is one reason why I desired you would not ascribe {innate} gravity to me. That gravity should be innate inherent & essential to matter so that one body may act upon another at a distance through a vacuum without the mediation of any thing else by & through which their action or force {may} be conveyed from one to another is to me so great an absurdity that I beleive no man who has in philosophical matters any competent faculty of thinking can ever fall into it. Gravity must be caused by an agent acting constantly according to certain laws, but whether this agent be material or immaterial is a question I have left to the consideration of my readers.[13]

For his part, of course, Newton firmly believed that the active agent was immaterial and divine.

As much as he tried, Newton was unable to maintain his resolution to keep hypotheses out of his official scientific account. Years later, in 1713, he inserted his famous commentary called the "General Scholium" into the second edition of the *Principia*. In the Scholium, he hypothesized that "This most elegant system of the sun, planets, and comets could not have arisen without the design and dominion of an intelligent and powerful being."[14] He further commented that "He rules all things, not as the world soul but as Lord over all."[15]

In one of his letters to Bentley, Newton made the following statement that has tantalized ever since: "There is yet another argument for a Deity which I take to be a very strong one, but till the principles on which tis grounded be better received I think it more advisable to let it sleep."[16] Newton never shared what this argument is.

Although his life seemed enviable, in 1693 Newton was living through his "black year." Despite his increased contact with people, Newton remained jealous of his privacy, so the events leading up to this dark time in Newton's life remain a mystery. In September of that year, he suddenly sent two bizarre letters, one to former Royal Society president Samuel Pepys, the other to Locke. In his letter to Pepys he wrote:

> I am extremely troubled at the embroilment I am in, and have neither ate nor slept well this twelve month, nor have my former consistency of mind . . . I never designed to get anything by your interest, nor by King Jame's favour, but am now sensible that I must withdraw from your acquaintance, and see neither you nor the rest of my friends any more, if I may but leave them quietly.[17]

We are left without a context here and so can only speculate what Newton is talking about. His letter to Locke is even more disturbing:

> Being of opinion that you endeavored to embroil me with
> woemen & by other means I was so much affected with it
> as that when one told me you were sickly & would not live I
> answered twere better if you were dead. I desire you to for-
> give me this uncharitableness.[18]

Again, we are hearing only one side of a conversation, perhaps a conversation that Newton was having with himself.

At any rate, these letters came out of nowhere, surprising both of their recipients, who, rather than taking offense, immediately worried that their friend was indeed ill. Thankfully, Newton recovered quickly, for he soon wrote to Locke, explaining:

> [T]he last winter by sleeping too often by my fire I got an ill
> habit of sleeping & distemper which this summer has been
> epidemical put me further out of order, so that when I wrote
> to you I had not slept an hour a night for a fortnight together
> & for 5 nights together not a wink. I remember I wrote to you
> but what I said of your book I remember not.[19]

Newton scholars have puzzled over the cause of Newton's crisis. Some have attributed it to exhaustion, the result of working intensely on unifying his various studies into a coherent whole. Others speculate that Newton was suffering from mercury poisoning. He was still experimenting in alchemy, and mercury poisoning can cause insomnia, paranoia, and memory loss.

But one theory has gained special attention for its sensationalism: Newton's illness was caused by a repressed desire for a young Swiss mathematician, Nicolas Fatio de Duillier (who was a friend of Huygens). Of course, just like contemporary views on the friendship between the Bible's Jonathan and David, this is pure speculation. To be sure, the two men were close friends, but it seems that Newton merely felt a responsibility for the troubled Fatio. David Brewster reported that Fatio's physical and spiritual health were poor and that Fatio consulted Newton on both. Their correspondence indicates that they were close enough to discuss the possibility of living near one another. And Locke suggested that they both come live at his home in Essex. None of these men roomed together, however, robbing us of delightful stories of bachelor mischief.

A genuine cause of Newton's sleeplessness may have been one of the unsolved problems of the *Principia*. Newton still could not mathematically describe the slight perturbations of the moon's orbit. He knew that the moon's deviations from his theory of orbital motion were the result of the sun's gravitational attraction on the moon and earth. We now know that this "three-body problem" has no exact solution. Newton was able to approximate a solution, but that is a far cry from his goal. He later said that "his head never ached but with his studies on the moon."[20]

Another, related, source of his headaches was the Astronomer Royal, John Flamsteed. To tackle the moon problem, Newton needed more—and more accurate—observational data. Flamsteed was a proficient astronomer, and in 1694, Newton requested the Royal data. Flamsteed was flattered: "Mr Ns approbation," he wrote, "is more to me then the cry of all the Ignorant in the world."[21] He was, therefore, forthcoming, but not entirely without hesitation. Because the government underfunded the observatory at Greenwich, Flamsteed bought equipment with his own money, and thereby felt that the observational data was his private property. He therefore demanded that Newton keep the data secret. Flamsteed was planning to publish all his findings in what would amount to his magnum opus.

When Newton later asked for more data, Flamsteed stalled. But Newton was in earnest. He must have that data. The perturbations of the moon's orbit was—perhaps literally—driving him mad. The more Newton demanded, the more Flamsteed resisted. Sometimes Flamsteed trickled some small bit of data to Newton, keeping their struggle alive. Newton would sometimes respond with rudeness, but eventually tired of his interchange with the sickly and temperamental Flamsteed. In 1695, Newton simply stopped responding to Flamsteed's letters. It was a tried-and-true solution.

Newton eventually gave up on the moon problem, resulting in a further retreat from natural philosophy. Perhaps Newton sensed that it was finally time to make a change, to move on to things more suited to his age and temperament. Conceding defeat in his battle with the three-body problem, Newton decided that Cambridge held little more for him. In 1696, after thirty-five years in Cambridge, he moved to London. He was fifty-three, and his serious study of science had come to an end. Newton kept one important tie with Cambridge: he remained the Lucasian Professor of Mathematics, holding the position in absentia for five years. He severed this last tie in 1701, resigning both his professorship and his fellowship.

14

ABOUT THE KING'S BUSINESS

By 1696, England was in a genuine financial crisis. Its currency—primarily coins—was a mixture of older hammered coins and newer coins produced by machines. The older coins were inexact and easy to counterfeit. Clippers, too, were a problem. They would trim a tiny unnoticeable sliver of gold or silver from the edges of the older coins. Done with enough coins, these filings could be melted down and sold. Newer coins had ornamented edges to prevent clipping.

The government put one of Newton's friends from Cambridge, Charles Montague, in charge of the problem. In 1695, Montague asked England's leading intellectuals for advice, including John Locke, Christopher Wren, and Newton. Montague eventually decided—and Parliament agreed—that England must remove all the older, hammered coins from circulation, replacing them with newer, machined coins—an enormous undertaking. Furthermore, declared Parliament, counterfeiting and clipping were now crimes of high treason, punishable by death.

Montague, aware that Newton was interested in one of London's government positions, secured for him a position as warden of the London Mint. It isn't clear whether Montague wished for Newton to play a role in the recoinage. His letter to Newton indicated that it was merely a sinecure—a comfortable position with a considerable salary, some prestige, and very little responsibility. The warden's position, Montague said, "has not too much business to require more attendance than you may spare."[1] Newton immediately accepted and moved to London within the month. On May 2, 1696, he took his oath as warden, swearing that he would, among other things, never reveal the carefully guarded secrets of the government's coining process.

In recent years, the wardens had been merely figureheads. The real authority—and the larger salary—lay with a nominally lower position, the master of the Mint. Thomas Neale was master at the time, and, unfortunately, was falling asleep at the wheel.

Newton threw himself into the recoinage operation, taking up Neale's slack—and everyone else's. This was simply Newton's way, and it wasn't going to change now. He began by learning everything he could about the Mint, its history, its operations, and its responsibilities. As usual, he indexed the information, organizing and categorizing it. His alchemy background, with its study of metals and their properties, had tailor made him to be in charge of coining. He mastered a new domain of knowledge and then used this foundation, yet again, to overhaul the system.

At the Mint, Newton's daily contact with people markedly increased. As warden, he oversaw manual workers, as well as other administrators who were scarcely used to being supervised. They were scarcely used to doing anything at all. Now, everyone found themselves expected to perform, and up to Newton's standards. This situation seemed designed specifically to create a conflagration. Newton—the only child, the loner, the professor who spent his entire life in thought—would hardly be someone to successfully oversee an institution of humans engaged in practical matters. But Newton—in a remarkable transformation—became a highly effective administrator, and he turned the Mint around during his three-decade tenure there.

The Mint was located in the London Tower, and, therefore, so was the warden's house. But the living conditions near the Tower were cramped and industrial, so Newton found a house elsewhere, on Jermyn Street, where he would live for the next decade. To the delight of his biographers, he decorated his house almost entirely in crimson: crimson drapes, crimson hangings, and a crimson mohair bed. As far as we know, crimson held no deep significance for Newton other than he simply liked it (although, the legendary Philosopher's Stone, one of the quarry after which Newton hunted his entire life, was said to be red).

During the recoinage, which lasted until 1698, the Mint was feverish with activity. Extra horses were brought in to drive the overhauled machinery, and the Mint ran from 4 a.m. until midnight every day. Newton wasn't in attendance for all of those hours, but his day was long and tiresome nonetheless. It was just like old times.

Except now he was famous. Even foreign political leaders were aware of his achievements, some of them asking specifically to meet with Newton when visiting England. In 1698, Peter the Great, czar of Russia, met with Newton while on a tour of the West. While in England, he wanted to see its shipyards, the Mint, and Isaac Newton.

One day Newton arrived home, tired, around four in the afternoon. Waiting for him was a letter from the president of the Royal Society, none other than his friend Montague. Montague was forwarding a message from the Continent. Johann Bernoulli, one of Liebniz's disciples, had issued a challenge "to the sharpest mathematicians flourishing throughout the world."[2] The challenge was a mathematical one: to determine the fastest trajectory that an object could take traveling from point A to a lower point B not directly below A. The task was essentially to find the fastest path of a roller coaster.

Tensions between Bernoulli and Newton were still high from when Bernoulli had accused Newton in 1696 of stealing mathematical secrets from Leibniz. Newton was still waiting for Bernoulli's apology. (He apparently never received it. In 1721, he wrote that "Bernoulli wished to have my picture; but he has not yet acknowledged publicly that I possessed the method of fluxions and moments in 1672."[3]) This new challenge was directed at Newton. Bernoulli—and Leibniz—wished to show that Newton was not as adept at mathematics as Leibniz. After a month had passed and Bernoulli had received no response from any of Europe's mathematicians, he extended the deadline (Leibniz himself said he needed a few more weeks) and sent the challenge directly to the Royal Society to ensure that Newton received it. According to Newton's niece, Catherine Barton, when Newton opened the letter, he "did not hesitate straightaway to attack the problem, indeed he did not sleep til he had solved it which was by 4 in the morning."[4]

Newton sent the solution to Montague the next day, and it was published anonymously in the *Philosophical Transactions*. When Bernoulli saw the solution, he said he easily recognized it as Newton's, as one recognizes "the lion by his claw."[5] It is unclear whether Leibniz bothered to finish his own solution. Newton, for his part, did not enjoy being tried: "I do not love . . . to be dunned & teezed by forreigners about Mathematical things."[6] Nevertheless, he wouldn't back down from a challenge.

At the Mint, Newton's responsibilities included more than making coins. Another of his duties was to apprehend and prosecute counterfeiters and clippers. He had unsuccessfully petitioned to be excused from such a "vexatious and dangerous"[7] job, but he was actually a master detective. He organized a network of spies and informers stationed in taverns and prisons. He purchased special disguises. He even had himself appointed justice of the peace. His interrogations were so effective that, on some accounts, records of them were destroyed. Under Newton's watch, incidences of counterfeiting and clipping dropped to astonishingly low levels.

Newton was a master of evidence, highly skillful at collecting the right kind of data. He had dedicated his entire life to the delicate relation between evidence and conclusions, and now he used his familiarity to remarkable effect. The defendants were no doubt surprised at how much Newton knew about their affairs. Many of them—the ones not immediately hanged and quartered—naturally held a deep grudge, and Newton's life was sometimes threatened. One of Newton's informers heard a prisoner, Francis Ball,

> complain of the Warden of the mint for severity against Coyners and say Damne my blood I had been out [of prison] before now but for him . . . and Witfield who was also there in prison made answer that the Warden of the mint was a Rogue and if ever King James came againe he would shoot him and . . . Ball made answer God dam my blood so will and tho I don't know him yet Ile find him out.[8]

Newton's initial concern was justified, but threats, rather than deterring him, only increased his dedication to justice. Newton did not like to be threatened. And in the end, many who threatened him were themselves having second thoughts about it.

One of the most dangerous coiners Newton faced was William Chaloner. To Chaloner, coining was an art, and through it, he had become wealthy and influential. Even his tongue was silver, and he used it to make trouble, while keeping himself out of it. He was ruthless. Once he convinced printers to publish pamphlets praising former King James. Chaloner immediately turned the printers in for a £1,000 reward, an enormous amount of money. The printers were executed, and Chaloner boasted that he had "funned" the government out of £1,000.

Chaloner tried to "fun" Parliament by claiming that the Mint had counterfeited coins. Newton was furious at the charge and gathered enough evidence to convict Chaloner of high treason. Chaloner swore that he "would pursue that old Dogg the Warden to the end so long as he lived."[9] Unfortunately for Chaloner, one of Newton's spies relayed the message. In the face of his execution, Chaloner begged Newton to show mercy. In a wretched letter to Newton, Chaloner wrote:

> Most mercifull Sir . . .
>
> O dear Sir no body can save me but you O God my God I shall be murderd unless you save me O I hope God will move yor heart with mercy and pitty to do this thing for me I am
>
> Yor near murderd humble Servant,
> W. Chaloner[10]

Newton couldn't have let Chaloner go if he had wanted to. But of course, the point is moot: Newton didn't want to.

Although Newton never again immersed himself in scientific studies, his interest never vanished entirely. In 1699, he finally showed up at the Royal Society. The recoinage was over, so the pressure at the Mint had been relieved. At one of the meetings, he showed the Society a sextant he had invented. At the next meeting Hooke—who was now very sick—claimed he had invented it. Newton returned to the Society only after Hooke died in 1703.

The rumblings of yet another controversy were felt when Fatio published an oblique attack on Leibniz's integrity regarding the invention of the calculus. Leibniz responded by saying that Newton himself said that they had *both* invented the calculus. Newton, however, denied ever saying such a thing. For the moment, however, the dispute lay dormant.

When Thomas Neale, the ineffectual master of the Mint,

died in 1699, Newton asked to replace him. In theory, warden was a higher position than master, but not in practice. Newton was granted his request and in 1700 was sworn in as master, an office he would hold until his death.

Moreover, the Mint had made him a wealthy man. According to Conduitt, although Newton "always lived in a very handsome generous manner," he did so "without ostentation or vanity, always hospitable & upon proper occasions gave splendid entertainments."[11] London life apparently suited him, although he could apparently get his fill of culture. He reported to Stukeley that he attended only one opera: "the first act, said he, I heard with pleasure, the 2d stretched my patience, at the 3d I ran away."[12] We shouldn't be surprised, however; he also called poetry "a kind of ingenious nonsense."[13]

Throughout the years, Newton had helped support his mother's side of the family. After his half sister Hannah's husband died, Newton gave financial help. Then, perhaps around 1700, one of Hannah's daughters, Catherine Barton, came to keep house for Newton in London. We do not know whether Hannah was having trouble with Catherine or if she simply wanted to increase Catherine's prospects. In any case, the latter would be no problem. Newton's niece was lovely, intelligent, and charming. Jonathan Swift, a close friend of Catherine's, said of her once, "I love her better than any one here."[14]

Before long, Catherine became the object of Charles Montague's affection. Montague was now Lord Halifax and styled himself as something of a ladies' man. Though we do not know the exact nature of Catherine's relationship with Montague, it has attracted significant attention over the years.

Most agree, however, that the £25,000—an enormous sum— that Montague left to Catherine in 1715 suggests an affair. In his will Montague said:

> These Gifts and Legacies, I leave to her as a Token of the sincere Love, Affection, and Esteem I have long had for her Person, and as a small recompense for the Pleasure and Happiness I have had in her Conversation.[15]

Voltaire was one of Newton's greatest admirers but also an incurable gossip. He couldn't help but infer that Catherine was the reason Montague supported Newton's appointment to the Mint: "Fluxions and gravitation would have been of no use without a pretty niece."[16] Newton, however, was appointed to the Mint long before Montague ever set eyes on Miss Barton. But we can be fairly certain that she and Montague were lovers. Flamsteed mocked Montague's claim that he left Catherine money "for her *excellent conversation*."[17]

Another enticing mystery, this one concerning Newton's own love life, is found in one of Newton's letters to Catherine. He mentions a woman: "My Lady Norris thinks you forget your promis of writing to her, & wants a letter from you . . . I am Your very loving Unkle."[18] There is also a surviving letter from Newton to Lady Norris. Her third husband had died, and Newton suggested that she not spend her remaining years grieving in "a melancholy life among the sepulchres."[19] Newton continued:

> The proper remedy for all these mischiefs is a new husband, and whether your ladyship should admit of a proper remedy

for such maladies, is a question which I hope will not need much time to consider of . . . and therefore since your ladyship likes the person proposed, I doubt not but in a little time to have notice of your ladyship's inclinations to marry, at least that you will give him leave to discourse with you about it. I am, Madam, your ladyship's most humble, and most obedient servant.[20]

David Brewster, Newton's nineteenth-century biographer, made a plausible case that the "person proposed" is Newton himself, the phrase "a quaint and not uncommon form of expression to avoid the use of the first person."[21] One thing we know: Newton and Lady Norris never married. On his deathbed, Newton confessed to his doctor that he was a virgin.

A FEW LAST FIGHTS

ooke's presence at the Royal Society had kept Newton away. But in 1703, Hooke died after a long and painful illness. Scholars, however, have found no evidence of Newton's sorrow. Nor have they looked for it. Newton immediately returned to the Royal Society. The Society elected Newton its president that same year, an office he held until his death.

It had been three decades since Newton had sent the Society his discoveries on light. Since that time, however, membership and finances had slumped in tandem. The Royal Society was a shadow of its former self. The two previous presidents had been politicians, merely figureheads, not natural philosophers. Neither of them attended the Society meetings, allowing the Society to drift aimlessly. Newton, however, took immediate control and established order—Newtonian order. Stukeley wrote:

Whilst he presided in the Royal Society, he executed that office, with singular prudence, with a grace, & dignity conscious of what was due to so noble an Institution . . . There were no whispering, talking, nor loud laughters, if dissensions arose in any sort, he said, they tended to find out truth, but ought not to arise to any personality. every thing was transacted with great attention, & solemnity, & decency. nor were any papers which seemed to border on religion, treated without proper respect. indeed his presence created a natural awe in the assembly; they appear'd truly as a venerable *consessus Naturæ Consiliariorum*, without any levity, or indecorum.[1]

And unlike his predecessors, he attended nearly every meeting until his health began to fail him two decades later. Newton was the exact opposite of recent presidents, investing not only his time in the Society but his money too.

Hooke's death also provided Newton the opportunity to publish once more. Newton had intended, at various times, to publish his findings in optics. Yet he had always changed his mind at the last minute. In 1704, however, he unveiled his complete theory of light and color in the *Optics*. In the introduction, Newton explained that he kept most of his optical research hidden all these years "to avoid being engaged in disputes."[2] Now that Hooke was gone, there was less chance of that.

The *Optics* contained mostly first-person narrations of his experiments and very little mathematics. It was, therefore, accessible to a much wider audience than was the *Principia*. Locke, for example, read it just before he died and, unlike his reading of the *Principia*, happily understood it all.

Although the *Optics* was not nearly as controversial as the *Principia*, it still contained topics that drew the Cartesians' fire. These attacks weren't aimed at the experimental or mathematical results—it was very difficult to argue with those. Rather, the targets were metaphysical, relating to explanations and causes. Although Newton kept his metaphysical hypotheses out of the main sections of the *Optics*, he decided to include them in a series of "Queries" at the end of the book. In these "Queries," Newton discussed the nature of ether, gravity, inertia, hidden forces, and God's relation to the cosmos. The "Queries," of course, presented his anti-Cartesian views, so the Cartesians were not impressed. The famous Cartesian philosopher Nicolas Malebranche commented, "Though Mr. Newton is no physicist, his book is very interesting."[3]

But the accolades mounted nevertheless, even outside natural philosophy. King William had died in 1702, and his sister-in-law, Princess Anne, succeeded him. Anne, a Protestant, was the daughter of James II, the Catholic king Newton had openly opposed in the Alban Francis incident. And Newton, as master of the Mint, designed her coronation medal. In April 1705, Newton traveled to Cambridge, where Queen Anne was to knight him during the traditional royal visit. On the evening of the festivities, after dinner—and in the same hall Newton served food as a sizar—he swore lifelong fealty to the crown. Surprisingly, Westfall said, Newton was not knighted for his contributions to science—or his service at the Mint. Rather, it was to ensure his election to Parliament, which would maintain bipartisan balance. The plan failed, however—Newton lost the election, and his Parliamentary career ended. One consolation was that Newton's knighting thoroughly annoyed Flamsteed, who afterward referred to Sir Isaac as "SIN."

The queen aided Newton another way in his ongoing

dispute with Flamsteed. Newton still did not have Flamsteed's data, which he needed to complete his lunar theory for the second edition of the *Principia*. Queen Anne no doubt knew about Flamsteed's reluctance to hand over the data from Greenwich. This data, after all, was the government's data—the *queen's* data. In 1710, she commanded that Flamsteed relinquish the observations and that the Royal Society oversee the observatory. Flamsteed obeyed, but hesitantly. He then openly complained that Newton had robbed him of the fruit of his labors. According to Flamsteed's account, Newton responded by calling him names, the least offensive being "puppy."[4] Newton, according to all accounts, went on to remove most of the occurrences of Flamsteed's name from the *Principia*. Flamsteed would die an embittered man in 1719. Succeeding him as Astronomer Royal was another of his hated enemies, Edmund Halley. And so Flamsteed's personal property—his data and equipment—all fell into his adversaries' hands. Death was better.

In 1710, Newton was confronted with another problem. Two years earlier, his successor to the Lucasian professorship, William Whiston, began to openly teach anti-Trinitarian views, which he likely learned from Newton. Whiston thereby violated Cambridge's rule that professors were to refrain from teaching anything not in compliance with Anglican doctrine. There was an important distinction between what a church member believed and what that member taught. Whiston, in propagating his heterodox beliefs, opened himself up to censure and, in 1710, was forced to resign his position as Lucasian Professor. Newton apparently took this as a personal affront—a betrayal—and his relationship with Whiston quickly cooled.

Newton had, after all, put his reputation on the line by recommending Whiston to succeed him. Whiston should have respected the difference between holding a view and indiscriminately spreading it. Newton had.

Along with the *Optics*, Newton published two important mathematical works, and for the first time in print, fully revealed his method of fluxions. He also made sure to mention that he had discovered the method in 1666. To support his claim of priority, he published his early correspondence with Leibniz.

Leibniz returned fire in 1705 by anonymously suggesting that Newton had actually learned the method from him and simply renamed it, dressing it in different notation. Newton's supporters published a counterstrike in the *Philosophical Transactions*, returning the compliment. Leibniz's own supporters were naturally indignant. The benches cleared, and thus began Newton's last big controversy. At first, the primary combatants backed away, allowing others to do the fighting. It became the most famous intellectual property dispute in history.

In 1711, Leibniz, who was also a member of the Royal Society, asked the Society to investigate the development of the calculus. The Society obliged and formed a committee to look over "old letters and papers."[5] The next year, in 1712, the committee concluded that Newton had first discovered the calculus ("by many years"[6]) and that Newton's version was simply better all around. In 1713, the Society published its report, along with the evidence supporting the committee's conclusion. Newton was its author.

Naturally enough, the report failed to settle the issue. Only after Leibniz's death did the fighting subside. But the wounds took decades to heal. England and the Continent, turning their backs to one other, walked away, murmuring. Skirmishes continued for another century.

History, however, has adjudicated the dispute. The jury's findings are that Newton was the first to discover the calculus (in 1666), a decade before Leibniz—but Leibniz was the first to publish. In 1686, Leibniz's paper *A New Method for Maxima and Minima, and Also for Tangents, which Stops at Neither Fractions nor Irrational Quantities, and a Singular Type of Calculus for These* had introduced the term "calculus" as well as our standard notation. And though Leibniz learned at least *something* of the method from Newton, Leibniz formulated the bulk of his own invention himself.

The scope of the dispute reached beyond mathematics into philosophy—in particular to the issues that Newton discussed in his "Queries" of the *Optics*. In *Theodicy* (1710) Leibniz had criticized the theory of gravity, charging Newton with reintroducing hidden qualities and miracles into philosophy. The fundamental difference between Newton and Leibniz originated with their very concept of natural philosophy. Newton, we saw, limited natural philosophy to the realm of experiments and mathematics. Experiments and mathematics, however, could not take natural philosophy where Leibniz wished it to go. Leibniz wanted to include metaphysical hypotheses in natural philosophy—he wanted explanations and fundamental causes. Given this difference, they could never agree. Publicly, Newton remained inside his restricted view of science; Leibniz, on the other hand, wanted to step outside to settle things.

Actually, Newton was never directly involved in the ensuing philosophical debate with Leibniz. Newton's personal correspondence with Leibniz was limited to mathematics. Rather, Samuel Clarke played Newton's part in the philosophical debate. Clarke was Newton's pastor and one of his closest friends. He had given the prestigious Boyle lectures in 1704 and 1705 and was now England's leading metaphysician (what we would today call a "philosopher"). Queen Anne had been Clarke's patron, but upon her death in 1714—and the ascension of George I—Princess Caroline assumed Clarke's patronage. Clarke met weekly with the princess, debating philosophy and theology.

Leibniz had tutored Caroline prior to her becoming princess of Wales and was concerned that Clarke would corrupt his former pupil with Newtonian philosophy. In 1715, Leibniz wrote criticizing the "English" philosophy, saying that in England:

> Natural religion itself, seems to decay very much . . . According to their doctrine, God Almighty wants to wind up his watch from time to time, otherwise it would cease to move. He had not, it seems, sufficient foresight to make it a perpetual motion.[7]

Leibniz was uncomfortable with Newton's belief that God is constantly involved in the upkeep of the universe. It suggested to Leibniz that God was an incompetent engineer—and a micromanaging one at that.

Caroline, wishing to hear Newton's side, showed the letter to Clarke, sparking one of the most famous philosophical discussions in history: the Leibniz-Clarke correspondence. Throughout the debate, Clarke most likely consulted closely with Newton. After all, the two lived only a block from each other. At the very least, however, Clarke's letters were entirely consistent with Newton's views, and the Leibniz-Clark correspondence is seen as the Leibniz-Newton correspondence.

As is often the case in debates, the real goal was the audience's allegiance. Neither Clarke nor Leibniz was going to change his mind; Caroline, on the other hand, was on the fence. She had been impressed with Clarke's arguments: "Mr. Clarke's knowledge and his clear way of reasoning have almost converted me to believing in the vacuum." She later said, "It is for you to lead me back into the right way, and I await the answer which you make to Mr. Clarke."[8] These were the stakes.

Caroline was the liaison between the men, receiving their letters, and sending them on. The debate continued until Leibniz's death the following year, and lasted for five rounds. Leibniz again criticized Newton's theory of gravity. He claimed that it went against the fundamental principle of philosophy that nothing is without a cause. Of course, Newton's theory did no such thing. And this Leibniz knew. Leibniz was actually concerned with what the cause might be: "But if [Newton] posits that the effects [of gravity] depend not on an occult quality but on the will of God or a hidden divine law, thereby he provides us with a cause, but a supernatural or miraculous one."[9]

The term "supernatural" would not have bothered Newton. He believed that God is continually active in the universe. Of course, just *how* God interacts with the physical cosmos, Newton wasn't sure. He once got himself into trouble by saying that space was God's *sensorium*—God's senses—by which he perceives everything in the universe, similar to the way we perceive our bodies. Newton corrected this by saying that space is *like* God's sensorium. Space isn't literally a part of God.

Leibniz failed to bring Caroline "back into the right way." Newton's view was a juggernaut that would eventually overrun the Continent as well as England. And when Newton's followers couldn't change the Cartesians' minds, they simply waited for the Cartesians to die. And when Leibniz sensed his turn approaching, he wrote to a friend, "Adieu the vacuum, the atoms, and the whole Philosophy of M. Newton."[10] Less than a month later, Liebniz bid his last adieu, succumbing to gout in November 1716.

In 1717, the young John Conduitt arrived at Newton's home to call upon his niece. Conduitt was young, at least compared to Catherine: he was not yet forty, and she nearly a decade older. He had attended Trinity College, after which he joined the military, enjoying a successful and prosperous career. Catherine was obviously impressed—she and John were soon married. Conduitt was one of the people closest to Newton during the latter's twilight years and eventually took over Newton's duties at the Mint when Newton's health began to decline.

Newton had enjoyed robust health and a long life—even by today's standards. His first serious illness was "an attack of the stone" (kidney stones) in 1722 at the age of eighty. This left him incontinent, and although his continence gradually returned, he never fully recovered. This incident must have reminded him that he had little time left, and he decided to work in earnest on a third edition of the *Principia*. There were, however, few substantive changes in the third edition. Newton simply had little left to give to natural philosophy. Rather, he spent his days working on theology, church history, and his ancient chronology.

He suffered another bout of kidney stones in 1724, which took a greater toll on his health. The next year he contracted a "violent cough and inflammation of the Lungs,"[11] continuing the inevitable downward trend. Catherine and John convinced Newton to move to Kensington, a suburb of London located just far enough away from the city's dangerously polluted air. Newton's breathing troubles subsided only to be replaced by a case of gout. Nevertheless, when he was advised that it would be better if he rode to church, rather than walk, he replied defiantly, "Use legs and have legs."[12]

Finally, in March 1727, Newton made a trip into London to visit the Royal Society. He felt and looked better than he had in years. The next day, however, a stone lodged in his bladder. But he was now as stubborn as he was old and waited a week before calling a doctor. At this point, the prognosis was grim—this stone was going to kill him. David Brewster recounted:

> From that time on he experienced violent fits of pain with very brief intermissions and though the drops of sweat ran down his face in these severe paroxysms, he never uttered a cry or a complaint, or displayed the least marks of peevishness or impatience, but during the short intervals of relief "would smile and talk with his usual cheerfulness."[13]

This was his final struggle. Last rites were called for; Newton refused them, possibly because he thought that the rite was an extrabiblical superstition. On Saturday evening, March

18, Newton slipped into a coma, never recovering. He died quietly and peacefully early Monday, March 20, 1727. He was eighty-four. The Royal Society's minutes report, "The Chair being vacant by the death of Sir Isaac Newton, there was no meeting this day."[14]

EPILOGUE

Newton left no will. By law, therefore, his estate at Woolsthorpe went to John Newton, a descendent of Newton's uncle. But, said the pastor at Colsterworth, John Newton was "a poor Representative of so great a man."[1] According to Gale Christianson, Newton's heir "gambled and drank his inheritance away, dying by accident when, after a round of drinking, he stumbled and fell with a pipe in his mouth, the broken stem lodging in his throat."[2] Although John Newton briefly enjoyed his inheritance, he despised his birthright.

As a rule, we, too, have squandered what Newton bequeathed. We believe that the limited scope Newton gave to science is still wide enough to embrace all there is. We are like a deaf and blind man who denies the existence of anything that he cannot detect with his remaining senses. Carl Sagan eloquently canonized our belief: "The Cosmos is all that is or ever was or ever will be." As of this writing, the current Lucasian Professor of Mathematics is the great physicist Stephen Hawking. Hawking once searched for a coherent and unified theory of the world, and in that sense followed in Newton's footsteps. It seems tolerably clear, however, that Hawking is out of step with Newton by believing that a unified theory of everything would be limited to a theory of the *physical* world. Newton also did not share the same opinion about the existence of aliens as Hawking does. As far as we know, Newton didn't believe in them; Hawking thinks it's likely they exist.

Newton certainly believed that there was more to reality than the physical cosmos, but he went farther. He believed that the *physical* world contains more than whatever falls within the ken of mathematics and observation. For Newton, even the physical world is supernatural. Keynes was right: Newton was a magician. Of course, the "magic" Newton believed in—he wouldn't have called it that—isn't impersonal. Its source is a Person.

Most physicists today don't believe in magic of any kind. But all of them behave *as if* they do. Take just one example. Jewish philosopher of mathematics Mark Steiner suggests that many physicists are schizophrenic—they deny the existence of a supernatural realm but use mystical symbols to probe the depths of the subatomic world. The discoveries of quantum physics, he says, relied on the manipulation of purely mathematical symbols, behind which there was no physical interpretation whatsoever. This, Steiner continues, borders on the magical.

> I say "magical" because the object of study of physics became more and more the [mathematical] formalism of physics itself, as though symbols were reality—and the confusion of symbols with reality is what characterizes much of what we call magic.[3]

Physicists focused on the mathematical runes, allowing mathematics alone to lead them where observation can never follow. But the mystery deepened when we learned that the mathematics took us into the atom, where classical Newtonian laws no longer work. The subatomic world behaves entirely unlike the macro world of everyday objects. And somehow the mathematics knew this—despite being developed for the macro world that follows different kinds of laws.

Physicists sense *something* mysterious is going on. Nobel Prize–winning physicist Eugene Wigner is staggered by mathematics' uncanny ability to "work." In his famous paper "The Unreasonable Effectiveness of Mathematics in the Natural Sciences," he wrote, "The miracle of the appropriateness of the language of mathematics for the formulation of the laws of physics is a wonderful gift which we neither understand nor deserve."[4]

Keynes was wrong—Newton wasn't the last magician. But he was the last one who knew that he was.

ACKNOWLEDGMENTS

I've been overwhelmed by the help and encouragement I've received while writing this book. The folks at Thomas Nelson have been superb. I'm particularly thankful for the cheerful and patient guidance from Joel Miller, Kristen Parrish, and Heather Skelton. They know what they're doing and are great at doing it. Also, my agent, Aaron Rench, has been invaluable. I'm privileged to have such an agent, who I suspect has genuine superpowers. Despite being educated at Oxford, he's far more than a mere academic. Lastly, I thank my wife, Christine, for proofreading every word of the manuscript, offering extremely helpful advice. To borrow from Anselm, Christine is that wife than which none greater can be conceived.

ABOUT THE AUTHOR

Mitch Stokes is a Fellow of Philosophy at New St. Andrews College in Moscow, Idaho. He received his Ph.D. in philosophy from Notre Dame under the direction of Alvin Plantinga and Peter van Inwagen. At Yale, he earned an M.A. in religion under the direction of Nicholas Wolterstorff. He also holds an M.S. in mechanical engineering and, prior to his philosophy career, worked for an international engineering firm where he earned five patents in aeroderivative gas turbine technology. He and his wife, Christine, have four children.

NOTES

CHAPTER 1

1. King's College Library, Cambridge, Keynes Ms. 130.03, p. 10v. See the Newton Project, http://www.newtonproject.sussex.ac.uk/view/texts/normalized/THEM00166.
2. R. S. Westfall, *Never at Rest: A Biography of Isaac Newton* (Cambridge: Cambridge University Press, 1980), 105.
3. G. E. Christianson, *Isaac Newton* (Oxford: Oxford University Press, 2005), 21.
4. G. E. Christianson, *In the Presence of the Creator: Isaac Newton and His Times* (New York: The Free Press, 1984), 4.
5. R. S. Westfall, *Never at Rest: A Biography of Isaac Newton* (Cambridge: Cambridge University Press, 1980), 141.
6. Ibid., 49.
7. D. Brewster, *Memoirs of the Life, Writings, and Discoveries of Sir Isaac Newton:* vol. 1 (Boston: Adamant Media Corporation, 2005 [1855]), 13.
8. Ibid., 14.
9. Westfall, *Never at Rest,* 59
10. J. Gleick, *Isaac Newton* (New York: Vintage Books, 2003), 3.
11. Brewster, *Memoirs of the Life, Writings, and Discoveries of Sir Isaac Newton,* 10.
12. Gleick, *Isaac Newton,* 14.
13. The Royal Society Library, London, Ms. 142, William Stukeley's Memoir of Newton , p. 34. See the Newton Project, http://www.newtonproject.sussex.ac.uk/view/texts/normalized/OTHE00001
14. Christianson, *In the Presence of the Creator,* 17.
15. Westfall, *Never at Rest,* 62.
16. The Royal Society Library, London, Ms. 142, William Stukeley,

Memoirs of Sir Isaac Newton's Life. See the Newton Project, http://www.newtonproject.sussex.ac.uk/view/texts/normalized/OTHE00001.

CHAPTER 2

1. Westfall, *Never at Rest*, 64.
2. King's College Library, Keynes Ms. 130.3, p. 21. See the Newton Project, http://www.newtonproject.sussex.ac.uk/view/texts/normalized/THEM00166.
3. Westfall, *Never at Rest*, 65.
4. D. Berlinski, *Newton's Gift* (New York: Touchstone Simon & Schuster, 2000), 13.
5. R. Iliffe, *Newton: A Very Short Introduction* (Oxford: Oxford University Press, 2007), 15.
6. Fitzwilliam Museum, Cambridge, Fitzwilliam Notebook, p. 3. See the Newton Project, http://www.newtonproject.sussex.ac.uk/view/texts/normalized/ALCH00069.
7. Ibid.
8. Iliffe, *Newton*, 4.
9. F. E. Manuel, *A Portrait of Isaac Newton* (Cambridge: Harvard University Press, 1968), 54.
10. King's College, Keynes Ms. 137, Letter from Nicholas Wickins to Robert Smith, p. 3. See the Newton Project, http://www.newtonproject.sussex.ac.uk/view/texts/normalized/THEM00035.

CHAPTER 4

1. Cambridge University Library, Cambridge, Add. Ms. 3996, p. 1. See the Newton Project, http://www.newtonproject.sussex.ac.uk/view/texts/normalized/THEM00092.
2. Ibid.
3. Christianson, *In the Presence of the Creator*, 59.
4. P. King, *The Life and Letters of John Locke* (London: Henry G. Bohn, 1858), 220.
5. Westfall, *Never at Rest*, 94.
6. King's College, Keynes Ms. 135, Humphrey Newton to John Conduitt, p. 1. See the Newton Project. http://www.newtonproject.sussex.ac.uk/view/texts/normalized/THEM00033.

7. King's College Library, Keynes Ms. 136 (part 3), p. 7. See the Newton Project, http://www.newtonproject.sussex.ac.uk/view/texts/normalized/THEM00158.

8. T. L. Heath, *The Thirteen Books of Euclid's Elements* (New York: Dover Publications, Inc., 1956), 3.

9. The Royal Society Library, London, Ms. 142, William Stukeley's Memoir of Newton, p. 55. See the Newton Project, http://www.newtonproject.sussex.ac.uk/view/texts/normalized/OTHE00001.

10. Ibid., 14. See the Newton Project, http://www.newtonproject.sussex.ac.uk/view/texts/normalized/OTHE00001.

11. Brewster, *Memoirs of the Life, Writings, and Discoveries of Sir Isaac Newton*, 24.

12. King's College Library, Keynes Ms. 129 (A), Fair copy of John Conduitt's Memoir of Newton, p. 8. See the Newton Project, http://www.newtonproject.sussex.ac.uk/view/texts/normalized/THEM00145.

13. Cambridge University Library, Add. Ms. 3996, p. 42. See the Newton Project, http://www.newtonproject.sussex.ac.uk/view/texts/normalized/THEM00092.

CHAPTER 5

1. Sunday 30 April 1665, http://www.pepysdiary.com/archive/1665/04/30/.

2. Westfall, *Never at Rest*, 38.

3. D. C. Lindberg and R. L. Numbers, eds., *God and Nature: Historical Essays on the Encounter Between Christianity and Science* (Berkeley: University of California Press, 1986), 322.

4. F. E. Manuel, *The Religion of Isaac Newton: The Freemantle Lectures, 1973* (Oxford: Oxford University Press, 1974), 49.

5. Ibid., 33.

6. Ibid., 22.

7. Ibid., 83.

8. S. Drake, ed. *Essays on Galileo and the history and philosophy of science,* vol. 1 (Toronto: University of Toronto Press, 1999), 53.

9. J. Gleick, *Isaac Newton* (New York: Vintage Books, 2003), 38.

10. Westfall, *Never at Rest*, 143.
11. Ibid., 139.
12. The Royal Society Library, Ms. 142, William Stukeley's Memoir of Newton, p. 15. See the Newton Project, http://www.newtonproject. sussex.ac.uk/view/texts/normalized/OTHE00001.
13. Brewster, *Memoirs of the Life, Writings, and Discoveries of Sir Isaac Newton*, 27.
14. Westfall, *Never at Rest*, 143.
15. Ibid.

CHAPTER 6

1. Fitzwilliam Museum, Cambridge, Fitzwilliam Notebook, p. 6. See the Newton Project, http://www.newtonproject.sussex.ac.uk/ view/texts/normalized/ALCH00069.
2. Westfall, *Never at Rest*, 179.
3. Fitzwilliam Museum, Fitzwilliam Notebook, p. 8. See http:// www.newtonproject.sussex.ac.uk/view/texts/normalized/ALC H00069.
4. I. Barrow, *The beauties of Isaac Barrow, selected from his writings by B.S.* (London: T. C. Newbt, 72, Mortimer ST., Cavendish So, 1846), 84.
5. Ibid., 58.
6. Manuel, *A Portrait of Isaac Newton*, 94.
7. Christianson, *In the Presence of the Creator*, 154.
8. Westfall, *Never at Rest: A Biography of Isaac Newton*, 202.
9. J. Gleick, *Isaac Newton* (New York: Vintage Books, 2003), 68.
10. Westfall, *Never at Rest*, 208.
11. King's College, Keynes Ms. 135, Humphrey Newton to John Conduitt, p. 2. See the Newton Project, http://www.newtonproject. sussex.ac.uk/view/texts/normalized/THEM00033.
12. P. Ackroyd, *Newton* (New York: Doubleday, 2006), 47–48.
13. Westfall, *Never at Rest*, 225.
14. Ibid., 217.
15. The Royal Society Library, Ms. 142, William Stukeley's Memoir of Newton, p. 61. See the Newton Project, http://www.newtonproject. sussex.ac.uk/view/texts/normalized/OTHE00001.
16. Westfall, *Never at Rest*, 212.

17. King's College Library, Keynes Ms. 130.10, pp. 3–4. See the Newton Project, http://www.newtonproject.sussex.ac.uk/view/texts/normalized/THEM00172.

18. http://royalsociety.org/page.asp?id=2176.

19. R. Society, *The record of the Royal society of London. 1897* (London: Harrison and Sons, 1901), 59.

20. Manuel, *The Religion of Isaac Newton*, 54.

21. Westfall, *Never at Rest*, 237.

Chapter 7

1. Westfall, *Never at Rest*, 239.

2. Christianson, *In the Presence of the Creator*, 157.

3. Ibid.

4. Ibid., 158.

5. Manuel, *A Portrait of Isaac Newton*, 138.

6. Christianson, *In the Presence of the Creator*, 155.

7. Ibid.

8. Westfall, *Never at Rest*, 243.

9. Ibid., 247.

10. Ibid., 250.

11. Ibid., 251.

12. S. H. Hartley, *The Royal Society, Its Origins and Founders* (London: The Invicta Press, 1960), 195.

13. Brewster, *Memoirs of the Life, Writings, and Discoveries of Sir Isaac Newton*, 155.

14. Ibid., 140.

15. Ibid.

16. Ibid., 141.

17. Ibid., 141. [emphasis in original]

18. Westfall, *Never at Rest*, 265.

19. Ibid., 263.

20. Ibid., 266.

21. Ibid., 281.

22. Brewster, *Memoirs of the Life, Writings, and Discoveries of Sir Isaac Newton*, 96.

23. King's College Library, Keynes Ms. 130.10, p. 4. See the Newton

Project, http://www.newtonproject.sussex.ac.uk/view/texts/normal
ized/THEM00172.

24. Brewster, *Memoirs of the Life, Writings, and Discoveries of Sir Isaac Newton*, 139.

25. Westfall, *Never at Rest*, 279.

CHAPTER 8

1. Westfall, *Never at Rest*, 280.

2. Brewster, *Memoirs of the Life, Writings, and Discoveries of Sir Isaac Newton*, 407.

3. Jewish National and University Library, Jerusalem, Yahuda MS 15.3 fol. 45r. See the Newton Project, http://www.newtonproject. sussex.ac.uk/view/texts/normalized/THEM00220.

4. Manuel, *The Religion of Isaac Newton*, 3.

5. Ibid., 21–22.

6. Westfall, *Never at Rest*, 312–13.

7. Jewish National and University Library, Yahuda MS 15.1 11r. See the Newton Project, http://www.newtonproject.sussex.ac.uk/view/ texts/normalized/THEM00218.

8. Manuel, *The Religion of Isaac Newton*, 58.

9. T. C. Pfizenmaier, "Was Isaac Newton an Arian?" *Journal of the History of Ideas* 58(1): 57–80, p. 61.

10. Ibid., 67.

11. Manuel, *The Religion of Isaac Newton*, 58.

12. R. S. Westfall, *Never at Rest: A Biography of Isaac Newton*, 333.

13. Jewish National and University Library, Yahuda Ms. 1.1, 14r, http:// www.newtonproject.sussex.ac.uk/view/texts/normalized/ THEM00135.

CHAPTER 9

1. B. J. Teeter Dobbs, *The Janus Faces of Genius: The Role of Alchemy in Newton's Thought* (Cambridge: Cambridge University Press, 2002), 7.

2. W. Applebaum, *The scientific revolution and the foundations of modern science* (Westport: Greenwood Press, 2006), 95–96.

3. Christianson, *In the Presence of the Creator*, 223.

4. Manuel, *The Religion of Isaac Newton*, 46.

5. Fitzwilliam Museum, Cambridge, Fitzwilliam Notebook, p. 3v. See the Newton Project, http://www.newtonproject.sussex.ac.uk/ view/texts/normalized/ALCH00069.

6. Christianson, *In the Presence of the Creator*, 214.

7. B. J. Teeter Dobbs, *The foundations of Newton's alchemy, or, "The hunting of the greene lyon"* (Cambridge: Cambridge University Press, 1983), 120.

8. Ibid., 195.

9. King's College, Keynes Ms. 135, Humphrey Newton to John Conduitt, pp. 2–3. See the Newton Project, http://www.newton project.sussex.ac.uk/view/texts/normalized/THEM00033.

10. M. White, *Isaac Newton: The Last Sorcerer* (Reading: Addison-Wesley, 1997), 146.

11. I. B. Cohen and G. E. Smith, eds. *The Cambridge Companion to Newton* (Cambridge: Cambridge University Press, 2002), 243.

12. http://www-history.mcs.st-andrews.ac.uk/Extras/Keynes_Newton.html.

Chapter 10

1. King's College Library, Keynes Ms. 130.8, p. 1. See the Newton Project, http://www.newtonproject.sussex.ac.uk/view/texts/normal ized/THEM00170.

2. S. Inwood, *The Forgotten Genius: The Biography of Robert Hooke 1635–1703* (San Francisco: MacAdam/Cage, 2005), 273.

3. Ibid.

4. Westfall, *Never at Rest*, 383.

5. Ibid., 384.

6. A. C. Grayling, *Descartes: The Life and Times of a Genius* (New York: Walker & Company, 2005), 2.

7. Westfall, *Never at Rest*, 377.

8. Gleick, *Isaac Newton*, 116.

9. Preface to "A View of Sir Isaac Newton's Philosophy" by Henry Pemberton. See the Newton Project, http://www.newtonproject. sussex.ac.uk/view/texts/normalized/OTHE00035.

CHAPTER 11

1. Westfall, *Never at Rest*, 405.
2. The following passages are all from King's College, Keynes Ms. 135, Humphrey Newton to John Conduitt. See the Newton Project, http://www.newtonproject.sussex.ac.uk/view/texts/normalized/THEM00033.
3. Gleick, *Isaac Newton*, 126–27.
4. Ibid., 127.
5. Brewster, *Memoirs of the Life, Writings, and Discoveries of Sir Isaac Newton*, 441.
6. Ibid., 111.
7. I. Newton, *The Principia: Mathematical Principles of Natural Philosophy* (Berkeley: University of California Press, 1999), 793.
8. Ibid.
9. King's College, Keynes Ms. 133, p. 10. See the Newton Project, http://www.newtonproject.sussex.ac.uk/view/texts/normalized/THEM00031.
10. King's College Library, Keynes Ms. 130.5, p. 2r. See the Newton Project, http://www.newtonproject.sussex.ac.uk/view/texts/normalized/THEM00168.
11. Newton, *The Principia*, 416.
12. Ibid.
13. Ibid., 417.
14. Ibid., 810.

CHAPTER 12

1. Cohen and Smith, eds., *The Cambridge Companion to Newton*, 291.
2. Newton, *The Principia*, 943.
3. M. Kline, *Mathematics: The Loss of Certainty* (Oxford: Oxford University Press, 1980), 73.
4. Newton, *The Principia*, 381.

CHAPTER 13

1. Newton, *The Principia*, 380.

2. Westfall, *Never at Rest*, 473.

3. Gleick, *Isaac Newton*, 152.

4. Ibid.

5. Ibid., 143.

6. Westfall, *Never at Rest*, 479.

7. Ibid., 489.

8. R. Ariew and E. Watkins, eds., *Modern philosophy: an anthology of primary sources* (Indianapolis: Hackett Publishing, 1998), 260.

9. Westfall, *Never at Rest*, 464.

10. G. Gjertsen, *The Newton Handbook* (New York: Routledge & Kegan Paul, 1986), 86.

11. Trinity College Library, Cambridge, 189.R.4.47, ff. 4A-5, p. 4v. See the Newton Project, http://www.newtonproject.sussex.ac.uk/view/texts/normalized/THEM00254.

12. Ibid.

13. Ibid.

14. Newton, *The Principia*, 940.

15. Ibid.

16. Trinity College Library, 189.R.4.47, ff. 4A-5, p. 5r. See the Newton Project, http://www.newtonproject.sussex.ac.uk/view/texts/normalized/THEM00254.

17. Brewster, *Memoirs of the Life, Writings, and Discoveries of Sir Isaac Newton*, 142.

18. Westfall, *Never at Rest*, 534.

19. Ibid., 536–37.

20. King's College Library, Cambridge, Keynes Ms. 130.7, p. 6v. See the Newton Project, http://www.newtonproject.sussex.ac.uk/view/texts/normalized/THEM00169.

21. Gleick, *Isaac Newton*, 154.

CHAPTER 14

1. Brewster, *Memoirs of the Life, Writings, and Discoveries of Sir Isaac Newton*, 191.

2. D. Berlinski, *Newton's Gift* (New York: Touchstone Simon & Schuster, 2000), 161.

3. D. Brewster, *Memoirs of the Life, Writings, and Discoveries of Sir Isaac Newton; Vol. 1* (Boston: Adamant Media Corporation, 2005 [1855]), 291.
4. Berlinski, *Newton's Gift*, 161.
5. Cohen and Smith, eds., *The Cambridge Companion to Newton*, 437.
6. Westfall, *Never at Rest*, 586.
7. Ibid., 568.
8. Ibid., 570.
9. Ibid., 574.
10. Ibid., 575.
11. King's College Library, Keynes Ms. 129 (A), p. 8v. See the Newton Project, http://www.newtonproject.sussex.ac.uk/view/texts/normalized/THEM00145.
12. Ibid.
13. Westfall, *Never at Rest*, 581.
14. Ibid., 596.
15. Ibid., 599.
16. Ibid., 596.
17. Ibid., 599.
18. Brewster, *Memoirs of the Life, Writings, and Discoveries of Sir Isaac Newton*, 213.
19. Ibid., 211.
20. Ibid., 211–12.
21. Ibid., 212.

CHAPTER 15

1. The Royal Society Library, Ms. 142, William Stukeley's Memoir of Newton, p. 73. See the Newton Project, http://www.newtonproject.sussex.ac.uk/view/texts/normalized/OTHE00001.
2. I. Newton, *Optics* (Chicago: William Benton, 1952), 377.
3. Gleick, *Isaac Newton*, 166.
4. Iliffe, *Newton:*, 120.
5. Gleick, *Isaac Newton*, 170.
6. Ibid.
7. Brewster, *Memoirs of the Life, Writings, and Discoveries of Sir Isaac Newton*, 285.

8. H. G. Alexander, ed., *The Leibniz-Clarke Correspondence* (Manchester: Manchester University Press, 1956), 194.

9. Christianson, *In the Presence of the Creator*, 530.

10. Gleick, *Isaac Newton* (New York: Vintage Books, 2003), 174.

11. King's College Library, Keynes Ms. 129 (A), Fair copy of John Conduitt's Memoir of Newton, p. 13v. See the Newton Project, http://www.newtonproject.sussex.ac.uk/view/texts/normalized/THEM00145.

12. Christianson, *In the Presence of the Creator*, 574.

13. Brewster, *Memoirs of the Life, Writings, and Discoveries of Sir Isaac Newton*, 392.

14. Berlinski, *Newton's Gift*, 2.

EPILOGUE

1. King's College, Keynes Ms. 134, Letter from Thomas Mason to John Conduitt, p. 1. See the Newton Project, http://www.newtonproject.sussex.ac.uk/view/texts/normalized/THEM00032.

2. Christianson, *In the Presence of the Creator*, 576.

3. M. Steiner, *The Applicability of Mathematics as a Philosophical Problem* (Cambridge: Harvard University Press, 1998), 136.

4. M. Colyvan, *The Indispensability of Mathematics* (New York: Oxford University Press, 2001).

The **CHRISTIAN ENCOUNTERS** seri

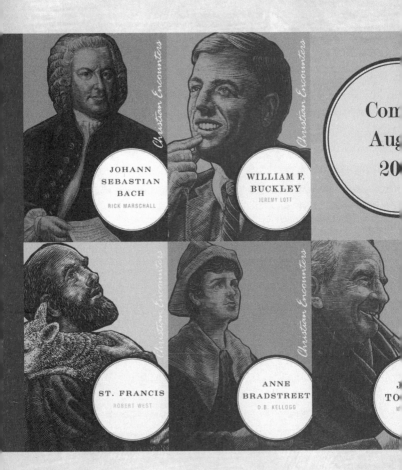

JOHANN
SEBASTIAN
BACH

RICK MARSCHALL

WILLIAM F.
BUCKLEY

JEREMY LOTT

Com
Aug
20

ST. FRANCIS

ROBERT WEST

ANNE
BRADSTREET

D.B. KELLOGG

J
TO

M

THOMAS NELSON
Since 1798